# Work

# Inequality

# Basic
# Income

Cameron Schrier Foundation • The William and Flora Hewlett Foundation
McCoy Family Center for Ethics in Society at Stanford University • National Endowment for the Arts

**Editors-in-Chief** Deborah Chasman, Joshua Cohen

**Managing Editor** Adam McGee

**Senior Editor** Chloe Fox

**Associate Web and Production Editor** Avni Majithia-Sejpal

**Poetry Editors** Timothy Donnelly, BK Fischer, Stefania Heim

**Fiction Editor** Junot Díaz

**Editorial Assistants** Tynan Stewart, Holly Winkelhake

**Poetry Readers** Andy Nicole Bowers, William Brewer, Ally Covino, Julie Kantor, Charlotte Lieberman, Becca Liu, Nick Narbutas, Diana Khoi Nguyen, Eleanor Sarasohn, Sean Zhuraw

**Publisher** Louisa Daniels Kearney

**Marketing Associate** Anne Boylan

**Outreach** Kira Brunner Don

**Finance Manager** Anthony DeMusis III

**Marketing Assistant** Jih-Chieh Yun

**Distributor** Disticor Magazine Distribution Services 800-668-7724, info@disticor.com

**Printer** Quad Graphics

**Board of Advisors** Swati Mylavarapu & Derik Schrier (co-chairs), Archon Fung, Deborah Fung, Richard M. Locke, Timothy Lyster, Jeff Mayersohn, Jennifer Moses, Scott Nielsen, Martha C. Nussbaum, Robert Pollin, Rob Reich, Hiram Samel, Kim Malone Scott

**Graphic Design** Zak Jensen

**Typefaces** Druk and Adobe Pro Caslon

**Permissions**
Tommie Shelby's "A Blow to Ghettoization" is adapted from *Dark Ghettos: Injustice, Dissent, and Reform* by Tommie Shelby. Copyright © 2016 by the President and Fellows of Harvard College. Used by permission. All rights reserved.
Jen Fitzgerald's "Glossary of Terms" and "Bargaining" are reprinted from her book *The Art of Work* (2016) with permission of the author and Noemi Press.
Jill Magi's "SPEECH" includes text adapted from Elizabeth A. Povinelli's *Economies of Abandonment* (Duke University Press, 2011).

To become a member or subscribe, visit: bostonreview.net/membership/

For questions about subscriptions, call 877-406-2443 or email custsvc_bostonrv@fulcoinc.com. For advertising questions, call 617-324-1325 or email ads@bostonreview.net.

*Boston Review*
PO Box 425786, Cambridge, MA 02142
617-324-1360

ISSN: 0734-2306

# Editor's Note

*Joshua Cohen*

WHEN YOU ARE EIGHTEEN YEARS OLD in the United States, you get a right to vote. That right comes to you regardless of sex, race, religion, class, or gender identity. You can lose the right in some places if you commit a felony, and there are lots of efforts currently underway to make it harder to exercise. But for now you do not have to earn it. Similarly with the right to a jury trial. Or our rights of association, religious worship, or expression. So the idea of universal entitlements is familiar.

When we extend the idea to economic resources, however, skepticism sets in. For many people, the idea of a universal right to a basic level of income seems deeply misguided. Many people, but not all. A long and intellectually diverse tradition, including Thomas Paine, Friedrich Hayek, and Martin Luther King, Jr., has embraced some version of a basic income. In 2000 *Boston Review* published an article by Belgian political theorist Philippe van Parijs explaining and defending basic income, often called UBI (universal basic income), that generated a wide-ranging debate. But with a few notable exceptions, attention to basic income has come from the world of theory, not the world of politics and policy.

Now something very different is happening. From Switzerland to eastern Kenya, from Manitoba to Oakland, the idea of a basic income is on the table as a serious policy idea and a focus of organizing efforts.

Why this growing interest? Partly for the same reasons that theorists have been drawn to basic income: it ensures everyone a claim on the benefits of common assets, such as land or other natural resources; gives substance to civil and political liberties; protects against extreme vulnerability; or, by cushioning against economic calamity, frees people to explore risky innovations.

But the attention to basic income also reflects a range of current concerns about income and job loss due to technology, deepening economic inequality, the sheer costs of administering conditional and in-kind programs, and the perceived vulnerability of conditional (means-tested) programs.

Leading the discussion, Brishen Rogers delineates a case for basic income. Focused on the United States, Rogers embraces a model in which a basic income guarantee is one component of a more comprehensive program, including a "revamped public sector and new and stronger regulations around work." For Rogers, basic income would provide an exit option from bad jobs, abusive relationships, and limited opportunities—in short, protections against political and economic subordination. A broader social-democratic setting is essential. Cut off from other essential policy initiatives, basic income could, Rogers argues, be a disaster.

The responses to Rogers's article explore the benefits basic income promises in fostering freedom and alleviating poverty and inequality, the need for basic income to be embedded in a more comprehensive program, and, if such a program is possible, whether basic income is really needed. As the debate about basic income moves from theory to practice, we hope that this *Boston Review* forum will model the serious policy and political debate that democracy depends on.

Cohen

In this forum, two additional issues emerge that have an important place in the debate about basic income—issues about work and power.

Some of the contemporary attention to basic income is animated by worries about a jobless future. In his fantastic book *Rise of the Robots* (2015), Martin Ford ties the case for basic income to job and income destruction driven by artificial intelligence. And not just destruction of repetitive work, but also the work of pathologists, radiologists, and legal researchers. Ford's argument is important but too speculative to be convincing. For the relevant future, we should assume a world in which people continue to work (often long hours) alongside machines.

Moreover, we should be wary of arguments for basic income as a substitute for income from work. Work is important to people, and not simply as a means to income. In his utopian novel *Looking Backward* (1887), Edward Bellamy imagines the world in the year 2000. He describes a system of rationally organized economic activity, with productivity unleashed through improved coordination and resources—including human capacities—fully employed for the common good. Aside from the implausibility of the scheme, the world of work in Bellamy's imagined future is depressingly dreary. As British designer and poet William Morris put it, "the true incentive to useful and happy labor is and must be pleasure in the work itself."

I know what Morris means. As a researcher I have spent lots of time in mostly Chinese factories over the past four years, watching people do very productive and very tedious assembly line work, with little apparent pleasure in the work itself. The work is not made more pleasurable when robots join the production team.

David Hughes wrestles with these issues about the importance of work in his ethnographic meditation on La Zarzuela, an Andalusian farming community now subsidized by windmills. He resists an easy celebration of the traditional work of farming, but he also hesitates to endorse the world of unemployed men and women, freed from toil, drinking beer and coffee in a community dominated by revenue-producing machines, unsure what to do with their time.

Alongside our conversations about basic income, then, we need a comparably serious discussion about how to create jobs that enable people—perhaps working alongside automated systems and robots—to find pleasure in the work itself. Of course having that conversation about decent work would be easier with a basic income in place. When people have greater income security, they are in a position to reject deadening work. And if they reject deadening work, then maybe some collective energy will go into figuring out how to enliven it.

The second issue is power. "Power," Frederick Douglass said, "concedes nothing without a demand. It never did and it never will." A basic income might create more decent conditions of work and would benefit working people. But the power of workers is now profoundly limited, both by income disparities and by the desperate state of collective organization (especially unions). Rogers has some ideas about labor law reforms, and the issue of organization and power is the focus of the essay by James Gray Pope, Ed Bruno, and Peter Kellman. The key to power, they argue, is the right to strike.

Of course, faced with our current calamities, discussions about ambitious political projects are hard to have. With voting rights themselves under assault, the idea that we should be thinking about a more *expansive* set of unconditional rights may seem delusional.

Or maybe not. We are in a fight about the future, and it is important to be clear about the larger purpose of that fight. Suppose, then, we think that we are aiming at a freer society, in which greater economic security reduces vulnerability and subordination, and a society in which people not only work for income but take pleasure in the work they do. That is not a bad start in describing a world worth fighting for.

Cohen

# From *Imperial Abhorrences (& Other Abominations)*

*Ammiel Alcalay*

## CONSUMER DEMAND

If you think of the
United States of America
as one huge nostril
a very long arm or
even a voracious mouth
reaching down to the
Andes and across the
fields of Afghanistan
the golden triangle
morphing into a shape
even Euclid couldn't
have imagined
then you're beginning
to get the picture

THINGS TO LOOK FORWARD TO:

After the
digital
drip
comes
the chip



R & D

What asshole
sitting in which
fucking airless
office came up
with driverless trucks?
Give me 40 acres,
motherfucker, &
I'll turn this
rig around.

Alcalay

# Basic Income in a Just Society

*Brishen Rogers*

"AMAZON NEEDS ONLY A MINUTE of human labor to ship your next package," read a CNN headline last October. The company has revolutionized its warehouse operations using an army of 45,000 robots and other technologies. Previously workers known as "pickers" would walk among shelves to find goods. Now robots bring the shelves to them; pickers select goods, scan them, and put them into bins; after robots whisk the shelves away. A network of automated conveyer belts then sends the bins to "packers," who spend just fifteen seconds on each, sealing boxes with tape that is automatically dispensed at the perfect length. "By the time you take an Amazon delivery off your stoop, walk into your home, find a pair of scissors and open the brown box," the story intoned, "you've already spent nearly as much time handling the package as Amazon's employees."

The story is hardly exceptional. Each week, it seems, another magazine, book, or think tank sketches a dystopian near-future in which new technologies render most workers unnecessary, sparking widespread poverty and disorder. Delivery drivers, the thinking goes, will not be needed when there are drones or autonomous cars staffed by robots, and Starbucks baristas and fast food workers will be redundant when a tablet can take your order and a machine can prepare it. Some even envision more skilled jobs at stake: robots repairing our homes, caring for the elderly, or nursing patients back to health. As President Obama warned in his farewell address, "The next wave of economic dislocations . . . will come from the relentless pace of automation that makes a lot of good, middle-class jobs obsolete."

An economic challenge of this magnitude requires ambitious solutions, and many in public debates have converged around a basic income. The idea is simple: the state would provide regular cash grants, ideally sufficient to meet basic needs, as a right of citizenship or lawful residency. Understood as a fundamental right, basic income would be *unconditional*, not means-tested and not contingent on previous or current employment. It would help sever the link between work and welfare, provide income security for all who are eligible, and perhaps mitigate growing inequality. It could also enable people to provide unpaid care work or community service, start new businesses, or get an education.

While this widespread attention to the problems of work and equality is welcome and overdue, and while a properly designed basic income would have many virtues, we need to be clear about the policy's justifications, merits, and limits. As noted above, basic income proponents often pivot off the threat of widespread technological unemployment. But students of capitalism have been predicting labor's demise ever since they identified and named "capitalism" itself. Is this time different? Consider what has happened at Amazon: warehouse robotics lowered prices and increased sales, and in early February the company announced plans to hire one hundred thousand more workers across the country.

Yet the news is still not good. Technology has transformed work in ways that have to do with political economy, not resource distribution. Amazon workers spend less than a minute per package because the company requires them to work at a furious pace, and it can afford to hire them by the thousands in part because it pays fairly low wages. Amazon also outsources many deliveries to third-party vendors whom it pays by the package, thus avoiding duties under wage per hour, workers' compensation, and collective bargaining laws. Increasing the pace of work and outsourcing are not new, of course, but information technologies make such efforts easier and more profitable. With computer analysis of barcode scans, for example, Amazon can track the efficiency of pickers, packers, and drivers without necessarily setting eyes on them. Technology is not a substitute for menial labor in this story but rather one among many tools to keep labor costs down by exerting power over workers.

This account changes the case for a basic income. Many of today's basic income proponents are libertarians and view the policy as a means of compensating losers, or as an excuse to repeal wage per hour or collective bargaining laws. Few are concerned about public goods, workers' and capital owners' entitlements within the firm, the power of various social groups, the ability of workers to organize collectively, and the question of what constitutes good work, not just jobs.

An alternative case for basic income draws from classic commitments to social democracy, or an economic system in which the state limits corporate power, ensures a decent standard of living for all, and encourages decent work. In the social democratic view, however, a basic income would be only part of the solution to economic and social inequalities—we also need a revamped public sector and a new and different collective bargaining system. Indeed, without such broader reforms, a basic income could do more harm than good.

This agenda will of course make zero progress during the Trump administration. But questions surrounding work and rising inequality are not going away. After all, Trump exploited fears of a jobless or insecure future in his campaign, signaling a return to our industrial heyday, with good-paying factory jobs implicitly promised to whites, men, and Christians. On the left, meanwhile, there is grassroots energy and momentum to think big and to address these issues head on, in all their complexity. But we still need a vision of good work and its place in our society, one that recognizes how our economy—and our working class—have changed dramatically in recent decades. I do not think for a moment that I have all the answers. But I do think an ambitious agenda around technology, work, and welfare can be a focal point and political resource for organizers, and perhaps even candidates, in the years to come.

CONSIDER THE LIFE OF A TRUCK DRIVER forty years ago versus today. In 1976 long-haul truck drivers had a powerful, if flawed, union in the Teamsters and enjoyed middle-class wages and excellent benefits. They also had a remarkable degree of autonomy, giving the job a cowboy or outlaw image. Drivers had to track their hours carefully, of course, and submit to weigh stations and other inspections of their trucks. But dispatchers could not reach them while they were on the road, since CB radios have limited range. Truckers would call in from pay phones, if they wanted.

No longer. Trucking companies today monitor drivers closely through "telematics" devices that gather and analyze data on their location, driving speed, and delivery efficiency. Some even note when a driver turns the truck on before fastening his seat belt, thereby wasting gas. As sociologist Karen Levy has shown, some long-haul trucking companies use telematics to push drivers to drive for all the hours permitted per day under federal law, at times waking them up or even overriding drivers' own judgments about whether it is safe to drive. UPS has used the technologies to reduce its stock of drivers, and many have noted the stress that "metrics-based harassment" puts on workers.

While the specter of self-driving vehicles is out there, this is the current reality for many drivers and will be for the foreseeable future. We have seen stunning advances in autonomous vehicles in recent years, but there is a vast difference between driving on a highway or broad suburban streets in good weather conditions and navigating narrow and pothole-filled city streets, not to mention making the actual delivery to houses, apartments, and businesses. As labor economist David Autor and others have argued, we are nowhere close to fully automated production or distribution of goods, since so many jobs involve non-repetitive tasks. In other words, the reports of the death of work have been greatly exaggerated.

Technological development is nevertheless altering the political economy of labor markets in profound ways. As we can see in the truck driver example, many firms are deploying information technologies to erode workers' conditions and bargaining power without displacing them.

And of course truck drivers are not alone. Many other firms today use advanced information technologies to push for more efficiency, in the process reducing workers' discretion, ultimately requiring them to work harder, faster, and for less. For example, where once taxi drivers' folk knowledge of the optimal path from A to B in a crowded city was a valuable skill, now Uber and Lyft can calculate the best route through GPS technology and machine learning processes based on data gleaned from hundreds of thousands of trips.

Other technological innovations make it easier—which is to say more efficient—to purchase labor without entering formal employment relationships and accepting the attendant legal duties. In the past firms tended to employ workers rather than contractors, or to pay employees above-market wages, in scenarios where it was difficult to train or monitor them. Workers who felt valued in this way would work diligently and remain loyal toward firms, ultimately reducing overall labor costs.

Again Uber's model helps illustrate. The company's app reduces consumers' and drivers' search costs significantly. Rapid scalability reduces Uber's costs of identifying and contracting with new drivers and riders; its GPS-based monitoring of its drivers enables it to know whether they are speeding or otherwise driving carelessly and whether they are accepting a sufficient number of fares; and its customer rating system enables it to manage an enormous workforce without managerial supervision. The net result is an economic organization of global scope based largely on contract where the firm disclaims any employment relationship toward its workers and therefore any employment duties toward them.

To be clear, there are powerful arguments that Uber drivers meet the legal test for employment, given the company's pervasive control of their work and its economic power over them. But given the ambiguities of current law, Uber has few economic incentives to bring drivers inside the firm, making them employees, or to extend them generous wage and benefit packages. Similarly Amazon's analytics help it to keep wages low: with barcode scanners tracking pickers' and packers' efficiency, the company does not have to pay workers as well to keep them motivated.

Finally, extensive data about market structures and consumer demand can enable firms to exert power over their suppliers or contractual partners, driving down costs—and therefore wages and conditions —through their supply chains. Walmart has long leveraged its unparalleled market data to estimate the lowest possible price suppliers will accept for goods, putting downward pressure on their profits and their workers' wages. Amazon does the same today, and franchisors such as McDonald's set prices and detailed product specifications for their franchisees.

Many firms today have substituted algorithmic scheduling for middle-managers' local knowledge, using data on past sales, local events, and even weather forecasts to schedule work shifts. A Starbucks employee, for example, has little schedule predictability since she is at the mercy of the algorithm, and a McDonald's worker can be sent home early if computers say sales are slow. This push to limit labor costs through finely tuned scheduling practices also alters workplace norms, since workers cannot appeal to a computer's emotions in asking for more or less time, a raise, or a slower pace of work. The net effect of all of this is that power in our labor and product markets is increasingly concentrated in a few hands.

Crucially such management techniques and new production strategies are often more efficient than the status quo. Amazon has undeniably lowered prices for goods through its use of automation. Similarly a recent MIT study calculated that just three thousand multi-passenger cabs using a version of Uber's algorithm could serve Manhattan's need for taxis. The potential benefits here are staggering, especially if coupled with a modern mass transit system: shorter commutes, less car ownership, less pollution, and more urban space.

But the line between innovation and exploitation is far from clear. While some workers will thrive as their unique skills and talents are rewarded by new technologies, many others will have less autonomy, less generous wages, less time for social connection, and unpredictable schedules. And under current laws, we can expect such trends to accelerate. Our labor and employment laws still envision the economy of the 1930s, which was dominated by massive industrial firms with hundreds of thousands of direct employees. Those laws rarely touch modern "fissured" work relationships such as Uber's relationship with its drivers, Walmart's relationship with its suppliers' workers, or McDonald's relationship with its franchisees' workers. Those laws also limit workers' ability to unionize or bargain effectively since they encourage bargaining at the firm or even plant level whereas today's modal workplace is growing ever smaller. Workers have fewer and fewer means to exert power on their own behalf.

HOW WOULD A BASIC INCOME impact workers and firms in this context? It would surely protect workers against the economic harms of unemployment and underemployment by giving them unconditional resources, and it would enable them to bargain for higher wages and to refuse terrible jobs. But a basic income would do little to reduce corporate power, which is a function not just of wealth but of the ability of firms to structure work relationships however they wish when countervailing institutions—such as a powerful regulatory state—are absent or ineffective. Yes, a basic income would make it easier for workers to organize and demand reforms—Andy Stern dubbed it "the ultimate permanent strike fund"—but the threat of termination or retaliation would still prevent many workers from protesting or striking in the first place.

And of course many have argued that a basic income would make minimum wage and collective bargaining laws less necessary, since workers' material needs would be met by the state. But cash benefits and reasonable wages are not morally equivalent. In Robert Solow's memorable phrase, the labor market is a "social institution" governed in part by norms of reciprocity and mutual respect. Workers often demand higher wages from larger and more profitable employers. And they work less diligently when they feel disrespected. So there is a major difference between a generous wage on the one hand and a meager wage supplemented with cash from the state on the other. Generous wages help make firms' economic responsibility roughly commensurate with their economic power. Meager wages signal disrespect, and state transfers are impersonal.

In fact, without labor market regulations in place, the impact of a basic income on very low-wage work could be disastrous. If a basic income were not extended to green card holders, guest workers, or "irregular" immigrants (those who enter or stay without authorization), such workers would be far cheaper to employ in menial jobs, at which point they would be permanently enshrined as a laboring underclass. (Currently minimum wage laws apply regardless of work authorization, on the grounds that differential treatment would undermine standards for all.) A basic income could even be designed to serve white nationalist ends. In fact, far-right European parties have often embraced the welfare state as a means of defending citizens against a purported tide of immigrants.

A standalone basic income also will not ensure equal access to quality education, health care, mental health care, housing, and transportation. Liberal markets systematically fail to provide such goods to the poor and working class, for the simple reason that they often are not profitable when provided on equitable terms. Giving cash to individuals to purchase them will not suddenly change matters.

POPULAR DEBATES HAVE LARGELY IGNORED these limits of a standalone basic income, an oversight that is not entirely accidental. As a tax-

and-transfer program, basic income would be consistent with a wide variety of political-economic systems, including neoliberal capitalism, social democracy, and various forms of socialism, but much of the basic income literature has a libertarian streak. On the right, Milton Friedman proposed a negative income tax in large part because he hoped it would reduce government bureaucracy. On the left, Philippe van Parijs's now-classic argument for the policy held it would maximize what he called "real freedom" better than standard welfare-state policies. And Silicon Valley's take exemplifies an "everyday libertarianism," which views market results, including pre-tax incomes, as presumptively fair.

Unlike many libertarians, basic income proponents accept the necessity and fairness of income and wealth taxation. But a basic income is still no cure for the moral ills of liberal markets. Since labor cannot be separated from workers, it will never be a classic commodity, and labor markets will never be stock exchanges for faceless buyers and sellers. Low wages carry a stigma that low bids for soybeans never will. In the long run, companies cannot treat workers or even consumers as line items on a balance sheet without risking a revolt. Uber is now paying a high price for ignoring this lesson. The company's flagrant disregard for our moral economy and its open embrace of a cutthroat, winner-take-all libertarianism made it a pariah in many quarters well before it faced allegations of a workplace culture of sexual harassment.

In my view, the more compelling arguments for basic income are rooted in commitments to equality as well as freedom. Take Thomas Paine's *Agrarian Justice* (1797), which prefigured the later case for social insurance. The earth, he argued, had been "the common property of the human race" in its natural state. Private property enabled the few to profit from the earth's resources, but all are entitled to compensation through a "citizens dividend." G. D. H. Cole updated Paine in the twentieth century, arguing for a "social dividend" on the grounds that all production is "a joint result of current effort and of the social heritage of inventiveness." Auto manufacturers did not discover electricity, after all, and Silicon Valley did not invent the Internet. Rather than a means of maximizing freedom, a basic income would help meet our duties toward one another.

A still more compelling case for basic income builds on Elizabeth Anderson's and Philip Pettit's (quite distinct) arguments that a just society must ensure that no group of citizens is subordinate to another. Extreme poverty causes subordination since it forces us to beg or to work at terrible jobs. Means tests are equally degrading since food stamps and similar programs tend to restrict what we can buy, again stigmatizing the poor. This argument is quite different from the libertarian case for a basic income since it does not view basic income as a replacement for the welfare state. Rather it asks basic income to serve a discrete and limited purpose: making sure nobody falls through the cracks.

And if one agrees that we need to root out subordination, we will need to do much more than pass a basic income. A just society would not just eliminate penury and then leave people to their fates. It would also strive for a fair distribution of *power*. This point strikes me as obvious, but we can miss it by focusing on unemployment and poverty. A society in which a few make decisions and the many take orders is an oligarchy, not a democracy.

This is what I mean by the "social democratic" case for a basic income: it would help build a post-industrial welfare state by alleviating dire poverty. But it is unlikely to pass and would do little good unless coupled with other efforts to ensure broadly dispersed power, including a substantially revamped public sector and new and stronger regulations around work.

THE PUBLIC SECTOR AGENDA should begin with a massive investment in human services. This would include primary, secondary, and higher education; childcare and elder care; health care; and mental health services. All of these are critical to human flourishing and economic growth, especially in a technologically advanced economy. There is also the added benefit that these sectors are among the least vulnerable to automation since they require interpersonal communication and human judgment: turning them into basic rights of citizenship would create millions of jobs.

Extensive job training and placement programs for unemployed workers would reduce the devastations associated with job losses. This should be coupled with a guarantee that the government will stand as employer of last resort, as William Darity and Darrick Hamilton have advocated. Classic WPA-style public works would be one option, but we might do more good by thinking locally: retrofitting houses and other smaller buildings for energy efficiency, as john a. powell and others have suggested, or building and repairing local parks and schools, or training unemployed workers for jobs in childcare, education, elder care, or health care. Some subset of the projects could be identified through participatory budgeting or other deliberative processes and carried out in partnership with local governments or organizations.

Then we should consider unconditional cash benefits in some form, ideally a generous basic income, especially if technological unemployment becomes significant. But we need to design it cor-rectly. If certain immigrants are denied a basic income, then we must establish a transparent pathway to citizenship and ensure that they enjoy generous wages. Currently many states restrict convicted felons from voting or collecting many public benefits. If that pattern holds with a basic income, that group could also become a pool of menial labor.

Paying for all of this would not be easy, of course, which is why it may make sense to take baby steps. Unconditional cash grants to parents, for instance, would go a long way toward alleviating poverty and would be less politically controversial than unconditional benefits for the able-bodied and childless. Or perhaps a participation income, in which citizens would be entitled to cash benefits on the basis of some qualified civic service each year, though this would be less desirable than a public jobs guarantee combined with other generous benefits.

As we wait for the politics to catch up with the policy, however, the "baby steps" approach can inch us closer to meeting social needs, developing a highly trained workforce and rebuilding faith in the public sector.

THEN THERE ARE THE NEAR-INTRACTABLE PROBLEMS of improving private sector work and limiting corporate power. Of course what makes work "good" is hard to define, in part because it is so dependent on social context and individuals' preferences. We look back fondly on the industrial era in part because manufacturing jobs delivered high wages and benefits, but those jobs only became "good" after workers organized and forced firms to raise wages and reduce hours. Manufacturing jobs were also physically and emotionally punishing, and factory workers' pride was often based on a perverse ethic of masculine suffering.

It is easier to say what *bad* work is. There is certainly no shortage of it these days: many workers earn low pay, have long or unpredictable hours, and are vulnerable to arbitrary treatment. Raising the minimum wage and reducing the standard workweek to thirty-five or even thirty hours would help. So would the public investments in human services discussed above, since those new jobs would require significant judgment (ensuring a degree of worker autonomy) and current law extends many democratic norms to the public sector already. A public jobs guarantee would give workers the security of knowing that an alternative always exists if a private-sector job proves unendurable.

The centerpiece of reform efforts should be the encouragement of collective bargaining between workers, their employers, and whatever other firms enjoy economic power over them. That will require reforms to bring our labor laws into sync with the reality of what work now looks like. Rather than requiring workers to organize shop by shop, we could encourage bargaining at the corporate level, such that all McDonald's workers, for example, would be in one bargaining unit, regardless of whether their restaurants are franchises or owned by the parent corporation. Better still, we could put all fast food workers nationwide in one bargaining unit empowered to negotiate with an association of fast food companies. Similarly workers could be granted bargaining rights with the firms at the top of their respective supply chains: Uber drivers would have bargaining rights vis-à-vis Uber, and Walmart and Target would have duties toward the workers who produce, process, and move goods to their shelves, including production workers, warehouse workers, farm workers, janitors, and many others.

This would work a major change in our labor law system, but the elements are already being built on the ground. On the company side, growing market concentration makes such bargaining quite plausible technically, if not politically. A national association of retail workers need only drive a settlement with Walmart, Target, Macy's, Gap, and a few others to raise standards. Where once taxi drivers would need to negotiate with hundreds if not thousands of medallion owners, now drivers can negotiate with Uber and Lyft directly.

Unions and other worker organizations have been dealing with these issues for decades and have developed workable models of organizing and bargaining that demonstrate proof of concept. For example, the Coalition of Immokalee Workers (CIW), an organization of farm workers in Florida, has pressed many major retailers and restaurants to join a "fair food program" under which they commit to paying more for produce and to rooting out slavery, corporal punishment, and other abuses in the fields. CIW succeeded despite having no collective bargaining rights at all and no legal employment relationship with the retailers and restaurants involved. They instead relied on high-visibility worker action, consumer boycotts, and creative media strategies.

Legal scholar Kate Andrias has argued that these efforts reflect an emerging model of unionism she dubs "social bargaining," in which workers demand that firms accept responsibility through their supply chains to a degree that exceeds the letter of the law. This strategy relies on public protest as well as more conventional union strategies—a kind of bargaining in the public green—and often utilizes state legislative power to backstop organizing efforts.

National legislation could encourage robust social bargaining in a variety of ways. Some states allow their departments of labor to constitute "wage boards" empowered to set wages within particular industries upon consultation with labor, firms, and the state. The federal government could follow suit, expanding the mandate of such boards to include issues of employee status, hours of work, and other basic standards. The federal government could also make it easier for workers to obtain union representation without enduring a contentious organizing process. Drawing from the Seattle legislation that established collective bargaining rights for Uber and Lyft drivers, firms could be required to disclose lists of workers to any worker organizations that meet basic indicia of independence and capacity.

It is crucial to emphasize the utility of social bargaining in today's economy. It would better reflect contemporary production relationships among firms, suppliers, and workers. It may even be relatively acceptable to large firms, insofar as it would seek to equalize wages across a sector and would not encourage detailed bargaining over worksite-specific minutiae, which employers have good reason to resist. And it could be carried out through organizations less formal than classic unions, which seem more appealing to contemporary workers. Of course, as with the public benefits outlined above, passing labor law reforms will not be easy. But how else can we realistically enhance workers' bargaining power?

THESE THREE POLICY SHIFTS—a basic income and other economic security guarantees, vastly expanded social programs, and new rules to encourage social bargaining—would supplement and reinforce one another. Better educational policies should help employers by ensuring a mobile, highly skilled workforce, and public health care and other social insurance would reduce the costs of employment. A basic income and a public jobs guarantee would enable workers to stand up for themselves more readily. Unions representing broad swaths of the precarious workforce would have incentives to push for a robust welfare state and even a basic income. Those unions could also reduce elites' domination of our politics, which may otherwise prevent implementation of a basic income, limit its generosity, or set it up to fail.

As many will realize, this institutional arrangement looks a bit like the Scandinavian "flexicurity" model—a portmanteau of "flexibility" and "security"—which combines high wages; extensive welfare and job training programs so workers can move between jobs; and relatively flexible employment policies that enable firms to hire, fire, and reassign workers at will. Such economies are quite open to technological innovation, but these institutions help ensure that its benefits are shared more equitably than they are in the United States. Not coincidentally, Scandinavian welfare states seem to be evolving toward a basic income, as the policy would fit nicely within flexicurity. But collective bargaining plays a crucial role in that system: without powerful unions, it is not clear that flexicurity would have developed in the first place, much less endured.

A basic income is a simple and elegant way to redistribute resources. But there are no simple, elegant solutions to complex political and economic challenges. A decent future of work and welfare requires a basic income—and much more.

# Will Basic Income Hurt the Cause?

## *Patrick Diamond*

THE LEFT HAS LOST ITS IDENTITY and is in a state of electoral and political crisis across the developed world. A basic income appears to offer a way out of the abyss for center-left parties since it creates the possibility of forging new coalitions of support between the "winners" and "losers" of globalization. The economic historian Robert Skidelsky insists that the two pillars that historically guaranteed stable incomes for the working class—full employment and comprehensive social security—are now glaringly inadequate. Moreover, a basic income purports to address a series of structural challenges, from automation and the growth of the precariat to demands for greater work-life balance and gender equality. In short, basic income offers a comprehensive vision for social welfare beyond the models that John Maynard Keynes and William Beveridge proposed in the late 1970s.

Nonetheless, the basic income schemes that are currently exciting political actors are scarcely a panacea. We need to be clear about a basic income's merits and its drawbacks. Brishen Rogers argues that economic security guarantees have to be combined with an expansion of the public sector and with rules that promote collective bargaining, increasing the relative power of labor in the wage-setting process. But while a basic income might be a big idea whose time has come, there are alternative strategies that stand a greater chance of winning over the public. And in the political struggle to create more egalitarian structures of work and welfare, it is reasonable to go further than Rogers, arguing that a basic income might actually hurt the cause.

First, basic income could set back the public debate about how to create more egalitarian societies, giving succor to the forces of state retrenchment. Indeed a basic income could amplify tax resistance and increase hostility to the welfare state. As Donald Hirsch has inferred, basic income involves "a very different tax settlement to the present one." In a climate of austerity marked by declining real wages, a basic income could well entail higher taxes on average incomes. Raising taxes is never politically popular, but to add insult to injury, these taxes would be used to fund a proposal that contradicted many citizens' notion of what is fair, flipping the concepts of contribution and reciprocity on their head. This is even more likely in countries such as the United States and the UK where there is a higher level of diversity and less sympathy for a universal social safety net.

In most western European countries, after all, voters agree that benefits and services should be directed toward those who need them most, especially children and pensioners. Moreover, work is valued as a social institution; it is widely accepted that a key function of the welfare state is to promote employment, a goal that is met very effectively in the Scandinavian countries. In other words, politically and culturally, Western societies are a long way from arriving at a "post-work" future. As long as paid work continues to be ascribed social value, those outside formal employment will be more vulnerable to isolation, poor health, and lower levels of well-being. A basic income or any measure that was perceived to promote worklessness would struggle to achieve public legitimacy. More importantly, it would risk souring the political discourse about radical measures to advance a more equal society—at a time when voters may be more amenable to it than at any point since the 1970s.

Second, a basic income could increase unemployment among vulnerable constituencies, exposing them to even greater precariousness. Research by Evelyn Forget in Canada and the United States in the 1970s showed that guaranteed income schemes reduced the working hours of "secondary earners," usually women, who were then more dependent on the principle breadwinner in the household. Feminist critics fear that basic income would lead to greater numbers of women dropping out of the labor market, or significantly reducing their working hours. Women would end up doing more unpaid domestic labor relative to men, making the household division of labor even more unequal.

Third, while a basic income has seemingly radical potential, it could be insufficiently transformative. Indeed basic income would simply trap the most disadvantaged in a cycle of inequality and precariousness from which there would be little prospect of escape. For an individual with an insecure job, trapped in low-paid work, and living in poor quality urban housing, it is hard to envisage how a basic income would substantively improve life circumstances. A basic income would compensate individuals for the effects of inequality, but it would absolve governments of responsibility for taking active measures to help those most exposed to "new" and "old" social risks.

Nor is a basic income a coherent answer to address the labor market inequalities that arise from technological change. The divisions that exist between high-skilled, high-wage workers doing non-routine jobs; non-automated workers employed in the low-wage services sector; and routine workers more exposed to the risk of unemployment remain intractable with or without basic income. A basic income would do little to address the unequal distribution of insecurity and precariousness. Because basic income is essentially a compensatory measure, it scarcely confronts the longstanding pathology of capitalist economies: vast inequalities in the distribution of assets, wealth, and ownership rights that are set to grow worse with the advent of new technologies.

Finally, a basic income could have a detrimental impact on existing social policy. The cost of basic income would mean that credible and evidence-based reforms of the welfare state and the labor market might become unaffordable. Most benefits and subsidies already in place would have to be renegotiated. Neoliberal advocates of basic income celebrate the idea because, in the words of Charles Murray, it would be a "replacement for the welfare state." Market liberals argue individuals could use their basic income to purchase services currently provided through the state: education, pensions, healthcare, unemployment insurance, childcare, and so on. Thus perversely (and contrary to the intentions of many of its advocates on the left), basic income might end up encouraging the marketization of the public sector, while limiting the funding available for social investment.

Basic income promises to cure a vast range of social ills through a single policy intervention. In reality a variety of carefully designed social policy programs are likely to have the greatest long-term impact. Rogers is correct to highlight the positive example provided by the Nordic welfare states offering high-quality provisions such as childcare, job training, and employment activation alongside relatively generous cash benefits. Those who seek a more egalitarian distribution of welfare and work in the advanced capitalist countries need to envision a "social investment" state that emphasizes high-quality, publicly funded services accompanied by more generous income subsidies to those in greatest need. And if they are going to be tempted by radical measures, they should focus instead on those proposals that explicitly challenge the unequal concentration of capital, wealth, and power.

The growing emphasis on "predistribution," for example, offers a fertile alternative to the basic income strategy. Like basic income, predistribution is a label for an idea with a long lineage in the radical tradition, stretching back to the eighteenth-century political philosopher Thomas Paine. The objective is to drastically reform markets to empower the wage-earning classes, "treating the root causes of inequality rather than attending only to the symptoms," as Jacob Hacker explains. The predistributive approach promotes the ideal of a property-owning democracy in which every individual has a stake in the market economy by virtue of being a citizen. Its aim is to provide a decent minimum income for all; to guarantee universal access to high-quality public services; and to create an equitable distribution of assets, capital, and wealth.

Three centuries after Paine published *The Rights of Man* (c. 1791), Western economies are still characterized by intractable inequalities in the distribution of wealth and inheritance. As Paine argued: "For all men being originally equals, no one by birth could have the right to set up his own family in perpetual preference to all others forever, and tho' himself might deserve some decent degree of honours of his contemporaries, yet his descendants might be far too unworthy to inherit them." Basic income has a Panglossian appeal, but the key task remains to find new routes to social justice and to fashion a more equal society by better understanding the world we are living in.

# Expanding the Goal of Innovation

*Annette Bernhardt*

TO STATE THE OBVIOUS, humans are the creators of new technology and can shape the path it takes (at least for now). Yet one common characteristic of basic income advocates, and indeed of progressives more generally, is a near-fatalistic acceptance of the current path of technological development. Either the topic is avoided altogether or automation is seen as inevitable. For a progressive movement that routinely challenges the market discipline of capitalism, this constitutes a striking retreat.

A truly progressive agenda around the future of work should therefore add control over technology into the mix: control of which technologies are developed and to what ends, and how they are incorporated into the organization of work and production. Moreover this agenda needs to expand beyond the current fixation on automation. Technology has many other equally important effects on work: for example, deskilling or upskilling existing tasks; shifting consumer demand toward new industries and new jobs; enabling outsourcing and the integration of a global virtual labor force; changing the job matching process; or disaggregating or aggregating workforces.

To be clear, this is a friendly amendment. In the future we will likely need some form of income replacement as well as Brishen Rogers's welcome call for a stronger public sector and more robust collective bargaining laws. But we should demand more.

What would it look like to claim our right as a society to govern technological development and its effects on workers and the labor market? Here are several possible strategies that move from less to more interventionist.

### Mitigation

IT IS TIME THAT PROGRESSIVES develop a robust and well-funded mitigation agenda. Basic income is one form of mitigation, but fleets of omniscient robots are decades away. There are plenty of near- and medium-term technologies whose effects we can anticipate or already see. Immediate forms of restitution could include industry- or occupation-specific funding pools and the technology equivalent of Trade Adjustment Assistance (education, training, and job placement for workers whose jobs are impacted by computers). Any number of business-side taxes could be leveraged for funding, including the robot tax endorsed by Bill Gates or a requirement that Uber pay into a fund for every self-driving car it puts on the road. And again, mitigation is not just about responding to automation. We might devise a deskilling tax, or mandatory retention and re-training laws when skill-changing technologies are introduced in the workplace.

Whatever specific tools we decide to use, a robust cost–benefit analysis of new technologies will be needed. Imagine that we include as metrics the number of workers displaced, the loss in their lifetime earnings, and the impact on their health and their children's earnings.

How would self-driving trucks fare under such an analysis? Even if the benefits still end up outweighing the full societal costs, at least we then have a metric by which to assess restitution. But perhaps a model of truck automation would emerge that preserves some percentage of the workforce to guide and manage the fleet.

## Collective bargaining

BECAUSE UNIONS ARE CURRENTLY FIGHTING for their lives, the first instinct within labor can be to obstruct technology. It is likely that important opportunities are missed as a result. In workplaces where unions still have enough density, the deployment of new technologies should become a topic of bargaining. In the 1960s and '70s, the longshoremen's union (ILWU) bargained over the adoption of shipping containers, thereby ensuring job security for incumbent workers, incentives for early retirement, and guaranteed pensions. But a lot of technological change is incremental and affects individual tasks rather than entire jobs. As a result there are many small decisions that cumulatively affect skill requirements, task mix, worker discretion, and promotion opportunities. Management consultants should not be the only voices guiding unionized employers when those decisions are made.

Technological change within one industry can also open up opportunities in another. For example, meal delivery apps are disrupting the food supply chain by delivering prepared meals and meal kits directly to consumers. But beneath the high-tech gloss lies surprisingly traditional work structures: scores of workers in large food processing facilities, many of them direct employees. Investigative reporting of Blue Apron's plants last year uncovered low wages and serious health and safety violations. If this new industry segment grows and thrives, it could offer fertile organizing ground.

A more ambitious approach is to figure out how to harness new technology for organizing. For example, alt-labor is exploring whether the aggregation provided by on-demand platforms can help to organize workers who had previously been isolated in disaggregated workplaces, such as domestic work. One barrier is that these platforms often do not allow worker-to-worker communication (which is no accident). Why not regulate labor platforms as a condition for receiving a business license, so that they would have to enable secure communication between workers and also agree to remain neutral if organizing results?

*Governance*

WHILE MITIGATION AND BARGAINING over impacts are important, ultimately the progressive goal should be governance: a seat at the table when decisions are made over which technologies are developed in the first place and in pursuit of which goals.

Governance can take several forms. One option is to control technology via direct regulation. For example, consider computer algorithms that result in discriminatory outcomes in lending, hiring, or sentencing. Law scholars are actively debating what type of anti-discrimination legal regime is needed to address these cases, which could potentially lead to regulating machine learning itself (since it is dependent on classification schemes). Product market regulation is another key arena. For example, how different would ride-sharing look if legislators had resisted Uber's lobbyists and classified Uber as a taxi company? Taxi apps would still have been developed but likely with different effects on drivers. The issue of who is able to access the big data generated by private sector firms is also receiving attention; often it is customers and workers contributing that data. Greater access by government could unveil underlying business models (such as predatory pricing) that might then be subject to regulation.

It would also be possible to take an active role in shaping technology via a multi-stakeholder model. The key insight is that there are multiple paths of technological development. Optimizing efficiency by reducing or eliminating human input is not the only path; within any given occupation or industry there are alternatives where technology works *with* humans to improve productivity. But how to shape what engineers call the design choice—augmentation vs. automation—is not yet clear.

Ideally we would establish mandated oversight structures that allow for multi-stakeholder decision making over what is developed. We would greatly expand the goals of innovation—to eliminating poverty, saving the planet, the full realization of every human being, the end of dangerous and back-breaking work, etc.—and maybe even insist that some amount of work has intrinsic value to humans. And we would harness the powerful fact that public dollars fund a lot of technological development, often in universities. As the saying goes, venture capital only funds the last mile.

Opportunities for this ambitious form of governance might be found in industries where there is a clear public interest. In the health care sector, for example, the path of technological development is not set in stone. Current attempts to introduce new technologies such as electronic patient records, automatic medication dispensers, and computer-assisted diagnosis have run into myriad challenges, some due to lack of federal standards, some due to competing goals, some due to unintended effects. A social bargaining model backed up by regulation could help pave the way to a health care system that uses technology to free up workers to deliver high-quality, patient-centered care.

IS ANY OF THIS FEASIBLE? Regulating and shaping technological change will require an enormous amount of power—over the private sector, over government, and over universities. But that is equally true of the basic income model and Rogers's extensions of it, which are predicated on there being sufficient political will to generate the needed revenue and change U.S. labor law. If we are willing to challenge capital to fund a basic income response to automation, then why not also try to govern technology directly?

The progressive case is that alternatives to shareholder capitalism exist and can thrive in the United States. By extension it should be possible to design and implement technology in a way that complements and values human work and is economically viable.

A final word: the tech sector is forging ahead without us. Last year Google, Facebook, Amazon, IBM, and Microsoft formed the Partnership on Artificial Intelligence to Benefit People and Society (Apple joined soon after), with the goal of establishing an ethics of artificial intelligence to ensure that it is developed with fairness and inclusivity, as well as transparency and an eye for privacy. Reportedly stakeholders from civic society will be invited, but in the end this is self-regulation. Who will be at the table to represent the voices of affected communities and workers, and how much power will they bring?

# A Blow to Ghettoization

*Tommie Shelby*

I AM LARGELY IN AGREEMENT with Brishen Rogers's discussion of the virtues and limits of basic income. I am persuaded that a basic income would be insufficient for economic justice, that it needs to be joined with a more robust set of public benefits, greater state regulation of labor markets and work conditions, and enhanced bargaining power for workers. I also agree that the most persuasive case for basic income is based on both freedom and fairness—liberty and equality. Rogers does not, however, explore how a basic income might advance the cause of racial justice. Here, as with much else, I think we can learn from Martin Luther King, Jr., who insisted in *Stride Toward Freedom* (1958) that economic injustice and racial injustice are "inseparable twins."

After the passage of the Civil Rights Act (1964) and the Voting Rights Act (1965), King turned his attention to the plight of the ghetto poor—that segment of the black poor who, because of past and ongoing racial and economic injustices, are confined to segregated and deeply disadvantaged metropolitan neighborhoods. Indeed, he moved with his family to a ghetto on the west side of Chicago. He called for a civil rights–labor alliance that fused the traditional antiracist aims of the black freedom struggle with the economic egalitarian goals of the labor movement. King supported unconditional basic income for the poor as part of a "Bill of Rights for the Disadvantaged." Such a measure was necessary, he thought, because of the negative impact automation was having on the employment prospects of ordinary wage laborers and because of the continuing economic marginalization of black urban poor. By extending King's vision to current realities and opting for basic income over means-tested welfare, we can see how basic income could reduce the suffering of today's black poor. In particular, basic income could significantly mitigate the burdens of ghettoization and mass incarceration.

One of the virtues of basic income that Rogers highlights is how it would sever the link between work and welfare. This would, by itself, advance the cause of racial justice. The linking of work and welfare has a long tradition in American culture and politics. Among both conservatives and liberals, work is often seen as a duty and as an indispensable basis for personal dignity. Joblessness, as a result, has become an influential explanation for why ghettos persist: the fact that so many among the ghetto poor do not work regularly, proponents of the explanation argue, accounts for why people in these communities often remain poor. Some advocates of this view maintain that jobless-ness has negative ramifications beyond mere income disadvantage. For instance, joblessness is said to increase crime and juvenile delinquency, to encourage welfare dependency and single-mother households, to undermine self-esteem, and to foster a self-defeating ghetto subculture.

Policymakers have responded by ending welfare as an entitlement, replacing it with strict time limits and work requirements for benefit eligibility, and cracking down on urban crime, and especially on the drug trade, pushing for long prison terms and aggressive enforcement measures. The idea is to encourage work in the licit economy by changing the incentive structure. But implicit in this policy response is the assumption that the black urban poor's reasons for refusing to work are insufficient. This assumption is widely held, quite old, and sometimes accepted by respected black leaders. But while I would not deny that high jobless rates in ghettos are worrisome and have far-reaching consequences, it does not follow that inducing or mandating work is the right solution to the problem of ghetto poverty. Indeed, many of the black urban poor have sufficient reason to refuse to work.

One of the basic problems with the current work-welfare regime is this: many of the ghetto poor who have submitted to its requirements nevertheless remain poor. They simply become part of the working poor, often serving the private needs of the well-off—performing the roles of maids, nannies, dishwashers, maintenance workers, and so on. Others fall back into poverty because of recessions and economic restructuring. And because many of the schools available to the ghetto poor are so substandard, they do not allow for opportunities to develop marketable skills, limiting upward mobility. Thus, when work requirements do not allow for skills enhancement or promotion to better paid positions, these requirements are reasonably interpreted as attempts by the affluent to profit by extracting burdensome and unrewarding labor from the weak and vulnerable.

Under these circumstances, mandating work to receive welfare benefits is disempowering—it ensures that the ghetto poor are a permanently exploitable class. To submit to an unjust and exploitative regime that stigmatizes and conveys contempt for poor black people is, for some at least, a fate worse than the ghetto. Many descendants of slaves embrace the imperative to resist race-based oppression, particularly those forms that are similar or related to past racial injustices. Blacks are therefore suspicious of and often bristle at any social arrangement that has the look or feel of race-based servitude. Perhaps some do not accept the jobs available because they believe that the basic structure of U.S. society is deeply unfair, and thus, on grounds of justice and self-respect, refuse to accommodate themselves to their low position in this racially and economically stratified social order.

Poor black mothers, for example, are often forced to accept employment in order to receive much-needed benefits. But the work available to them is often domestic service in the homes of affluent white families. By refusing this kind of work, they are resisting the ideological image of the mammy—the self-sacrificing, deferential, faithful, and obedient house servant—and its associated social roles. As Patricia Hill Collins has argued, a lot of the work in the contemporary service industry—preparing and serving food in restaurants, janitorial jobs and hotel housekeeping, and looking after kids in childcare centers—is reminiscent of traditional domestic service.

The symbolic meaning of such an arrangement (regardless of the conscious intent of those who support the work regime) is, I think, a sufficient reason for the most vulnerable and powerless segment of the black population to be defiant in the face of its demands. Apprehending the symbolic meaning of this work-welfare regime, some among the ghetto poor may (if they are able to) reject it as insulting.

There is considerable evidence that some Americans oppose welfare entitlement programs because they are prejudiced against blacks, with whom such programs are generally associated. A longstanding and deeply offensive stereotype about blacks is that they are lazy. The ghetto poor would also have grounds to refuse work, then, if they have a justified belief that their fellow citizens have erected a work regime because of racism, whether as a means to punish shiftlessness or as a paternalistic effort to correct habits of indolence.

High-poverty neighborhoods with few good employment options lead some residents, especially those unemployed for long periods, to consider securing income through unlawful means. Ghetto poverty creates desperation and feelings of shame, and some, seeking to escape the weight of their social conditions, resort to crime. As a result, many who reside in ghetto neighborhoods have been incarcerated. Upon release their felony records make it difficult for them to find work or housing, as it is not illegal to deny a person a job or an apartment because they have been convicted of a felony. Most convicted felons were already disadvantaged by their limited skills, low educational achievement, and lack of work experience, and they are not eligible for many forms of public assistance. The formerly incarcerated are thus among the worst off in ghetto neighborhoods. Families who depend on them for support are also made worse off by high incarceration rates and the treatment of ex-convicts.

Rogers rightly worries that if convicted felons were to be ineligible for basic income, they would likely become a permanent laboring underclass, forever stigmatized, exploited, and poor. But given the employment discrimination they face (particularly if they are black), many would turn, not to menial labor, but back to crime and so likely end up re-incarcerated, where a for-profit prison might still exploit their labor.

Given the history of slavery and Jim Crow—three and a half centuries of gross and far-reaching injustices—no one can plausibly argue that the current, racially skewed distribution of resources is entirely the result of just appropriations and fair market exchanges. Nothing approaching adequate reparations for slavery or Jim Crow have been offered to the descendants of slaves or the victims of the segregation regime. Given that contemporary ghetto poverty is plausibly explained, at least in part, by historical injustices in appropriation and transfer (what some term *structural racism*), it is far from clear that welfare conditional on work or the denial of public benefits to former felons is justifiable.

Therefore one of the strengths of basic income is that it would empower marginalized black workers by enabling them to refuse demeaning, insecure, exploitative, and low-paying jobs. They could do so without having to live in degrading forms of poverty and without having to bear the risks of the underground economy. Basic income would deal a real blow to ghettoization and mass incarceration. It would not solve all problems of racial or economic injustice. But any civil rights–labor alliance should seriously consider fighting for it.

# The Overdue Next Step

*Peter Barnes*

BRISHEN ROGERS ARGUES that basic income, though appealing, is not a one-stop policy solution. He is not against basic income per se; in fact he rather likes it. He is just against a standalone basic income.

Well, fine—who could disagree? No single policy can fix everything. But in making this particular argument, he overlooks an important distinction. At this time, when massive technological unemployment is an interesting future scenario but far from a sure or imminent reality, we should not be focusing on *basic* income. Rather, we should be focusing on *base* income, which would address a number of immediate problems while avoiding the pitfalls of the more ambitious iteration.

What is the difference between the two levels of universal income, and why does it matter? A *base* income of, say, a few hundred dollars a month does not have the same economic, political, and moral ramifications as a *basic* income of, say, $1,000 a month. The latter, at least in some places, offers enough to survive on; the former decidedly does not. And while the latter is a dream of many, it is far too expensive—and threatening to our work ethic—to be enacted in the United States any time soon. What is more, if it eventually does happen here, it will only be because it was preceded for many years by a universal base income. So let's focus on what is useful and possible in ten to fifteen years, rather than what is theoretical and, at best, several decades away.

The first advantage of a base income is that it has a proven American model to draw from. In Alaska, an oil-based Permanent Fund has paid yearly dividends to every resident (adult and child) since 1982. The payments have been in the vicinity of up to $2,000 a year. With more than three decades of data to draw on, an analysis by Ioana Marinescu of the University of Chicago shows that employment and wages in Alaska have followed the same trajectory as in comparable states without a universal income. The only exception is that about 2 percent of Alaska's work force appears to have shifted to part-time work, reflecting the added flexibility that extra income affords. And that is arguably a good thing.

On a national level, a base income would serve as both a springboard and a safety net for every participant in our fast-changing economy— like giving every player in Monopoly $200 for passing Go. It would supplement, but does not replace, labor income, and does so without judgment or stigma. It is grounded on the principle that, in a prosperous but volatile and wealth-concentrating economy, everyone has a right to some cash flow they can count on.

In practical terms, a national base income would be easy to administer. Eligible recipients (anyone with a valid Social Security number, which can include legal immigrants) would get equal amounts of money wired to their bank accounts or debit cards every month. People who don't need the extra income could use a check-off option to donate it to an IRS-approved charity, or simply not register in the first place.

A base income, it should be noted, has nothing to do with robots or artificial intelligence. It has a lot to do with enhancing every American's financial security, reducing their stress, and giving the poor and middle class a leg to stand on—the very opposite of what our economy does now.

A base income would have other benefits as well. It is an answer—perhaps the answer—to long-term economic stagnation, a trickle-up form of Keynesianism that would stimulate our economy through increased household spending.

Moreover, if funded by fees on unproductive activities such as pollution and speculation, it would help solve two other deep problems of twenty-first-century capitalism: climate change and financial instability. And it would not need to replace existing means-tested benefits, a regressive trade-off that conservatives favor but most progressives oppose. Indeed, fighting for a base income can go hand-in-hand with fighting for a bigger public sector, stronger collective bargaining rights, and a host of other policies. We can walk and chew gum at the same time.

Are there any downsides? The two leading objections to a full basic income are that it is frighteningly expensive (paying every American $1,000 a month would consume 20 percent of GDP), and that it would turn us into a nation of slackers. Neither of these critiques applies to a base income. Its cost would be on the order of 5 percent of GDP—the equivalent of the cost of Social Security—and its impact on the work habits of Americans would range from neutral to positive, as seen in Alaska.

Finally, there is the argument that a base income is the logical next step of the progressive path we have been on since the New Deal. Eighty-two years ago Franklin D. Roosevelt's Committee on Economic Security produced the report that led to passage of the first Social Security Act. The report itself went beyond security for the aged. It proclaimed:

> The one almost all-embracing measure of security is an assured income. A
> program of economic security, as we vision it, must have as its primary aim

the assurance of an adequate income to each human being in childhood,
youth, middle age, or old age—in sickness or in health.

The committee went on to say that, for reasons of political expediency, it was calling for immediate action only with regard to old age security, but it hoped that the rest of its vision would be implemented in the not-too-distant future. Much of it has, but not all. A lifelong base income, along with health insurance for all, are the overdue next steps.

# Basic Income Convergence

*Juliana Bidadanure*

IT WAS LUNCHTIME IN LONDON. I was trying to eat my fries and get ready for my afternoon talk on "The Future of the Left" when I overheard the men next to me grumbling something about universal basic income. They were discussing the recent referendum in Switzerland, where nearly 77 percent of voters opposed the idea of giving adults an unconditional monthly income of 2,500 Swiss francs.

The two men had been loudly disagreeing on various things for a while, but they were now very much agreeing on one thing: giving cash to everyone is a bloody stupid idea!

I was slightly taken aback, but mostly amused by the coincidence so I introduced myself as someone who was in town to give a talk on the subject that very afternoon. I asked why they so vehemently opposed the idea that everyone should have the unconditional right to be free from basic economic insecurity. Basic income, they conceded, is a beautiful sentiment, but completely unfeasible: any country that introduced it would get flooded with immigrants in no time.

This is a common objection to basic income. Nationals of countries without basic income, the argument goes, would have stronger incentives to move to countries with generous basic income policies, which would threaten the stability of the welcoming states and their capacity to deliver a generous basic income in the first place. An immediate solution to this pull effect "problem" would be for states to deliver a citizens' income rather than an income for all its residents. Under such proposals, noncitizens would not be entitled to the unconditional safety net until they themselves became citizens.

But as Brishen Rogers points out, a basic income only for citizens is a troubling proposal. Insofar as we are interested in basic income because we see it as an instrument that will free people from abject economic deprivation, it is morally dubious to exclude a group that contains some of the most marginalized and deprived members of society, leaving them even more disproportionally vulnerable to exploitation. As Rogers puts it, if non-citizens are excluded, "such workers would be far cheaper to employ in menial jobs, at which point they would be permanently enshrined as a laboring underclass."

Worse, basic income could be "designed to serve white nationalist ends," Rogers worries. The policy could be sold as part of a package including harsher anti-immigration policies. Prisoners and ex-cons could also be denied basic income, which would further entrench basic income as a right that privileges white Americans. This concern is not specific to basic income though. Far-right populist parties often embrace the welfare state in an exclusionary and xenophobic manner, proposing reforms that would protect the rights of the "deserving" poor over the rights of migrants (and their children) unduly free-riding on benefits.

The problem here is xenophobia, not basic income. For moral and political purposes, basic income should be asserted as a right of residency, not citizenship. But in order to do that, we need to address the issues of immigration and xenophobia head on.

First, it is important to note that the pull effect phenomenon associated with basic income may be overestimated. Up to this point, too few studies assess the theoretical foundation and empirical validity of this concern. No studies show convincingly that the decision to migrate to one country rather than another correlates to social protection systems. As Àlex Boso and Mihaela Vancea argue, "Once we control for other factors, the welfare magnet hypothesis does not seem to hold." So while it is plausible that basic income will have a pull effect, we cannot just assume that it will be huge, and we should not use the assumption to make exclusionary proposals.

Second, we must move beyond domestic basic income. Progressives should not be discussing basic income exclusively at the national level in rich countries when the causes and mechanisms of poverty are global and when absolute abject poverty is disproportionately found in developing countries. If we are going to talk about "the right to an income," that conversation must take place at the international level too.

That conversation may seem (and to a large extent is) far more utopian than the debate over whether we should have a basic income at the national level. Our conceptions of wealth redistribution are still largely constrained by institutional nationalism as well as a strong sense of exclusive solidarity toward co-nationals. So we seem to be a long way from a transnational basic income. And yet, the transnational basic income debate has already started.

There has been an evolution in the field of development toward cash transfers, with many initiatives seeing great success. Give Directly, for instance, is a nonprofit that facilitates unconditional cash transfers via mobile phone. They recently announced launching the largest ever basic income pilot in Kenya. Moreover, many countries in the Global

South—such as India, Namibia, South Africa, and Brazil—are actively discussing, experimenting with, or implementing versions of basic income. This suggests that developing countries are just as likely to move forward with some sort of basic income as are richer countries.

There are also a few existing regional and global basic income proposals, such as Philippe van Parijs's EU-dividend, Simon Blackburn's Global Pension and Youth Grant, and Thomas Pogge's Global Resources Dividend. All of these proposals could be funded through taxes on international financial transactions. Alleviating the economic insecurity that often motivates forced migration can in turn have an important effect on population flows.

Third, if we want to make sure that the basic income proposal that gets put forward or implemented is not a xenophobic one, then groups that defend the rights of migrants should have a central place in the growing basic income coalition. The Movement for Black Lives, for instance, which regularly shows its support for migrants, has recently endorsed basic income as part of their platform. So has Ai-Jen Poo, director of the National Domestic Workers Alliance, an organization that represents the interests of domestic workers in the United States.

As an egalitarian theorist, I find myself in broad agreement with Rogers's position that, from a progressive perspective, basic income is necessary but not sufficient to tackle growing inequalities. But I object to his lukewarm embrace of basic income as something that might marginally improve workers' lives, rather than a project with a critical political goal. Indeed, in some places, his lack of enthusiasm makes one wonder why we should push for one at all since it is so hard to win and only achieves so little.

From Rogers's basic message that a basic income is insufficient, we seem to slip into the view that it is somehow superfluous for progressive change—an avoidable part of a complicated package. Insisting that a basic income is insufficient in this manner often ends up unnecessarily sapping a rising enthusiasm for the policy for no good reason. This is unfortunate, since a basic income has unequalled potential to foster convergence between diverse grassroots movements. Few policies can help such different groups as domestic workers, truck drivers, stay-at-home moms, abused dependent partners, ex-cons, sex workers, starving artists, people who hate their jobs, people who love their jobs but need to reduce hours, volunteers, interns, students, poor pensioners, precarious workers, people who want to start an ecovillage, and so many more.

If the basic income movement is representative of all those voices, including groups that fight for the rights of migrants, we cannot only ensure the proposal is asserted as a right of residency (and avoid the dangerous drifts Rogers worries about), but the movement can also help federate those groups and be the cornerstone of a powerful alternative progressive imaginary, helping us move away from Trump's divided America.

# Reparations and Basic Income

## Dorian Warren

BRISHEN ROGERS IS RIGHT that a basic income will not solve all of the problems created by the political economy of American capitalism. It will not magically solve the collective action problem among workers and the powerless vis-à-vis corporate power.

But most proponents do not see it as a magic bullet. Many of us see it as one of several elements in a reimagined twenty-first-century social contract that provides economic security for all. And we get there via different political and strategic routes. Futurists and technologists come to the basic income idea via technology and automation. Libertarians come to basic income from arguments around efficiency and reducing the size of the state. Progressives come to basic income from a concern around non-domination, freedom, and redistributive justice.

I come to basic income from a very different political tradition: black politics with a focus on race and political economy. It is this tradition that led both Martin Luther King, Jr., and the Black Panther Party to argue for full employment and a "guaranteed income" fifty years ago. Though they wanted these specifically for African Americans, they hoped they would be made available to *all* Americans. Five decades later it is about time the rest of us caught up to their vision.

Black workers today face the exact same dual crisis of high unemployment and low-wage work that they did fifty years ago. The black unemployment rate is twice that of white workers at nearly every level of education. Thus one need not be only concerned with future trends to speculate that a basic income would help black Americans today, especially those who continue to be locked out of access to labor markets.

Rogers is spot on to warn us that basic income could be "designed to serve white nationalist ends." We know this from our own historical experience. Seemingly "universal" social policies, from the New Deal to the Great Society, have had intended and unintended consequences of maintaining or exacerbating existing racial and gender inequalities. Many supposedly "universal" policies ultimately were not.

But Rogers's rightful skepticism and warning about a white nationalist basic income comes down to a question of *political power*. President Franklin D. Roosevelt compromised on his New Deal programs because southern Democrats insisted on it. The race-based occupational exclusions of agricultural and domestic workers were ultimately included in Social Security, the National Labor Relations Act, and the Fair Labor Standards Act to appease political elites protecting the southern Jim Crow racial and economic regime over the protests of racial justice organizations. Black workers were excluded as a result of this previous iteration of white nationalism and populism. But advocates for a truly universal social policy did not give up, eventually winning racial inclusion in Social Security but not the other two major New Deal policies.

Similarly we should not limit our political imaginations about the promise of a basic income because of the very perilous questions around race, immigration, and exclusion. Quite the opposite. We should imagine a robust basic income that advances racial and gender justice while simultaneously addressing the ills of twenty-first-century capitalism.

I have argued that a basic income in all but a few forms—those that exclude the incarcerated or result in a net decrease in benefits—would benefit African American communities for the following reasons.

First, it would provide an individual-sustaining basic floor for returning citizens caught up in the criminal justice system.

Second, even an equal income could disproportionately benefit black Americans. White Americans earn more overall, so a greater percentage of their basic income would be taxed back. More importantly today's wealthiest Americans benefit either directly from African Americans' disadvantaged position in our political economy, or indirectly as a result of the cumulative benefits to our nation from centuries of exploiting black bodies. Black Americans either helped build the co-owned wealth of our nation (our infrastructure and banking, legal, and patent systems) or were denied access to our share of it (land, sky, and other natural resources). Even if African Americans receive an income equal to whites, tapping wealth hoarded by racist means and distributing it universally effectively amounts to targeted redistribution.

Third, a basic income would be an improvement on portions of today's current safety net. Some benefits, such as food stamps, are replete with paternalistic restrictions that rest on racist tropes about recipients and their consumption habits. Others, such as the Earned Income Tax Credit (EITC), are significantly tied to work, which is problematic when structural racism continues to create so many barriers to black employment. A basic income lacks these flaws.

The underlying assumption around welfare and entitlement reform has been that racial minorities do not want to work and that existing social policies provide "disincentives" to work. Basic income fundamentally decouples work from the economic right to basic needs and arguably bolsters individual-level bargaining power in the labor market. It also, by virtue of its universality, is less likely to be viewed as a program solely to benefit one racial or ethnic group. For sure, racialized attacks on cash grants will continue, but progressives are in a stronger position arguing for a universal program, knowing that it will in fact benefit African Americans greatly.

There is, in fact, a model of basic income which is not only acceptable but *preferable* to common proposals: the Universal PLUS Basic Income. It is identical to most basic income proposals but includes a pro-rated additional amount for black Americans over a specified period of time. The Universal PLUS Basic Income draws on the concept of "targeted universalism" in designing social policies. Such a proposal would take into account the historical and cumulative disadvantages of income, wealth, and inheritance afflicting black communities, and it would recognize that potential changes in the nature of work will disproportionately hurt black Americans. It would effectively function as reparations in a grand bargain with white America: all would benefit, but those who suffered through slavery and continuing racism in the economy would benefit slightly more.

Most importantly a campaign around a racially inclusive basic income is a potential opportunity for creating the political will within black communities and across racial and ethnic divides in American politics. Rogers, after all, suffers from the same limited theory of change with which he charges libertarian basic income supporters. How and under what conditions will the political will for his broad public sector program to advance economic security and human flourishing be created? Yes, there have been incredible victories by fast food, retail, and farm workers over the past decade to advance worker power, and these efforts are necessary but not yet sufficient to win national labor law reform.

But public opinion around economic redistribution has always been higher among black Americans relative to the rest of the population, and initial polling and focus groups around support for a basic income in the United States suggests this pattern still holds. Thus a U+BI proposal could become a bridge to the increasingly salient demand for reparations and reinvestment emerging from the Movement for Black Lives. And, if nothing else, it serves as a stronger starting progressive bargaining position in political fights over basic income. We are not yet at a moment to argue beyond basic income. We have to build the campaign to win it first.

# An Answer to the Wrong Question

*Diane Coyle*

ABOUT EVERY QUARTER CENTURY, as Brishen Rogers points out, accelerating automation seems to bring a wave of anxiety about the disappearance of jobs and a corresponding wave of enthusiasm for basic income. It happened in the 1960s and the early 1990s. It is happening again now. The machines will take all the jobs, the argument goes, and something must be done about it.

But Rogers is correct to emphasize that fears about the end of work have proven to be overstated. In both of those recent episodes, machines did kill some jobs, but created more as the economy grew and new occupations emerged. The arrival of automatic teller machines, James Bessen points out in his book *Learning by Doing* (2015), led to an increase, rather than a decrease, in the number of jobs for humans. Demand for banking services increased, and people carried out tasks other than mechanically handing cash to customers. The impact of automation for some individuals—those unable to retrain or find as work that paid as well—was terrible. But in the aggregate, the number of jobs increased. Since the anticipated mass unemployment simply did not occur, the introduction of a basic income proved unnecessary.

It is of course possible that this time is different, that the cleverness of artificial intelligence (AI) will really destroy jobs and that the economy will not display its normal adaptability. A much-cited study by Oxford University academics, for instance, claims that about half of all jobs in the United States and UK are at risk from AI during the next twenty years. But economists at the Organisation for Economic Co-operation and Development did a careful assessment of that research and argue that the proportion of jobs affected will be fewer than one in ten—bad enough but not apocalyptic.

This is not a call for complacency, however. Like Rogers, I see the changing economy as an enormous policy challenge. Past episodes indicate that governments have not yet figured out how to minimize the disruption costs when there is structural change in the economy from automation. I agree with Rogers that helping individuals make the transition in their own lives—through public sector investment in education and stronger worker protections—is a vital part of the puzzle. But I also contend that we should embrace new technologies to ensure the economy as a whole is growing and therefore creating demand for new activities.

The latter part actually requires *more* robots, installed faster. We need businesses to improve their productivity and sell innovative services and products attractive to consumers. The low productivity growth of the past ten years suggests there has been too little automation, not too much. Productivity is an abstract economists' term, but it is the driver of rising living standards over the long run; it means getting more services and products that people value out of the available resources. Machines make it possible by taking over routine tasks and saving time.

As Rogers illustrates, however, new technologies have changed the realities of business, and there are specific concerns about the behavior of the companies doing the automation. The big multinationals setting the pace on automation have gained a good deal of market power in several sectors of the economy. They use their economic heft to political ends, to ensure the regulatory framework and weak antitrust policy continue to support their position in the market and the economic rents they gain from that. They are adept at arbitraging different tax and regulatory systems to minimize the amount of tax they pay.

The existing framework of employment regulation and public policy is not structured to keep up with these new demands. Most importantly, as Rogers emphasizes, it is not designed to support individuals in a labor market consisting increasingly of big global corporations and contingent local work. For example, a minimum wage assumes the policy can be delivered through stable employers rooted in their community. But the old nation- and community-based social contract between businesses and citizens has crumbled.

We lack even the minimal data to understand how many people are working in this gradually emerging robot economy. For all the talk of the "gig" economy, there are no statistics on how many people rely on gig work, what they earn, and what they would like to be doing. Recent work by University of Maryland and Census Bureau economists points out that two sets of official U.S. figures do not even agree on the trend in self-employment. Data based on tax returns suggest it is rising, but data based on household surveys suggests that it has been falling. The former is probably more accurate, but there is unhelpful statistical fog (in all countries, not just the United States) in part because existing surveys are built around the conventional idea of the job and that structure is steadily disappearing. This makes it similarly difficult to gauge the effects of the new economy on benefits, pensions, and health insurance.

Looking at other countries' labor markets might help, however. Driving for Uber in the United States might be described as contingent: a few hours a week around one's domestic tasks, or as a second source of income. But in the UK, Uber is licensed as a taxi company and many of its drivers have switched from other cab companies. In Indian or African cities—or for that matter in the high unemployment suburbs of Paris—being an Uber driver is a pathway into the formal economy from a far more contingent existence as a day laborer, or being unemployed.

It is certainly not impossible to devise practical policies to tackle these challenges, but the task is immense and one governments have failed before. The legacy of failing the last generation of workers in industrialized states and regions is still with us—in declining towns, chronic ill health and drug abuse, substandard housing, disappointing educational outcomes, and low incomes. It is hard for adults to retrain at all, and especially when the fundamental skills needed in the workplace have changed so much. The education system (on both sides of the Atlantic) is failing miserably to equip children for the jobs of the future, so fundamental education is a big task ahead and one that is not on the political radar.

Rogers's call for a more robust public sector is spot on. We need measures for taxpayer-funded education and retraining; increased provision of public services; and perhaps even job guarantees for some redundant workers. Above all, though, we need constraints on the market power of corporations and their tax avoidance.

Perhaps these measures seem politically unrealistic, but they are certainly more realistic than a basic income. After all, many of them have been put into practice in the past.

Besides, a basic income is an answer to the wrong question. It addresses a hypothetical future problem of no jobs in place of jobs of the kind many people still do—such as driving trucks, or nursing patients.

Market economies can always adjust to create new kinds of work. We have very few horse-and-carriage drivers or dock hands these days, and many social media consultants and special effects designers for video games. If the robots take over those jobs in turn, humans will define other activities as work, impossible to foresee now. This is the kind of transition that has been occurring for a quarter of a millennium now, and it will occur again.

Given the uncertainty, however, basic income experiments in places such as Finland and the city of Utrecht in the Netherlands are to be welcomed. These will give economists some evidence to chew over, especially regarding the effect on work incentives, or the cost of such a large-scale program. But in the United States, at least for the foreseeable future, it is quite hard to envision enough voters being won over to a something-for-nothing option.

Skeptics of a basic income are right to point out its utopianism. What is needed now is less of the beautiful dream and more of the dirty realism. Get the data to understand people's job market alternatives and choices, work out how to regulate the actual labor market more effectively, and make a start on specific policies to re-tether the automating businesses to the societies out of which they are making their profits. And most important of all, continue to grow the economy to ensure new jobs—whatever form they take—are created.

# Real Freedom

*Philippe van Parijs*

ACCORDING TO BRISHEN ROGERS, "a decent future of work and welfare requires a basic income—and much more." With a piece concluded in this way, I am unlikely to have big disagreements. Even about the exact content of the "much more" we may well concur, if only because priorities are unavoidably different in different parts of the world. For the United States, Rogers proposes revamping the public sector and rejuvenating the collective bargaining system. In Europe, my own top priorities would include the reclaiming of our cities from cars and the proliferation of lifelong blended learning. Elsewhere in the world, priorities may be access to water, universal literacy, or the securing of civil peace. No hope of a sharp disagreement on this count.

Nor do I think we disagree about why basic income is needed. Alarmist forecasts about the impact of automation are undoubtedly a factor in the current unprecedented worldwide interest in basic income. But like Rogers, I do not believe in an inevitable rarefaction of jobs. In my new book with Yannick Vanderborght, *Basic Income:*

*A Radical Proposal for a Free Society and a Sane Economy*, we do not advocate basic income as a way of enabling the permanently unemployed to keep quiet and consume what the robots produce. Rogers mentions that some of the American advocates of a guaranteed income in the 1960s used the prospect of automation as their main argument. This argument is actually much older. To illustrate: I just received issue number 1182 (yes, 1182!) of *La Grande Relève des Hommes par la Machine* (The Great Replacement of Men by the Machine), a magazine founded in 1932 by French socialist Jacques Duboin, who was already pleading for a universal "social income" to avert an imminent and fatal crisis of underconsumption that would generate permanent unemployment.

The case for basic income does not rest on the assumption that human beings will be replaced by robots, but that does not mean that technological change is irrelevant. In complex interaction with economic globalization and with cultural trends affecting the employees' loyalty to their firm, the strength of trade unions or family stability, technological change is leading to a polarization of market earning power. Incomes are increasing for those who own capital and intellectual property rights, or who possess valuable talents and credentials. By contrast, there is now little hope of decent income for many of those whose skills are poorly valued by the market, who cannot learn new skills or move to areas in which their skills are more valued, and for many of those with family constraints that prevent them from working full time. In order to provide such as these with a sufficient income, one might think of more or less stigmatizing means-tested social assistance, of wage subsidies or of guaranteed public employment. But one can also think of an unconditional basic income. Rogers expresses his attraction to the latter in terms of equality, whether equality of status or equal share in the return on society's capital. In our book, we formulate our own principled preference for it in terms of real freedom, and we try to clarify the relationship between this justification and rival or complementary ones. I shall not do so here and focus instead on Rogers's main critique of standard defenses of basic income, namely that they are oblivious of capitalist power relations.

The power of each individual to say yes or no to a job, a power closely related to the notion of real freedom, has been present in the advocacy of basic income from its inception. Thus, in his 1871 *Catéchisme Populaire* (Populist Catechism), Joseph Charlier described the crucial advantage of the unconditional income for which he advocated: "It is no longer the worker who will have to bow before capital, it is capital, reduced to its true role of collaborating agent, that will have to negotiate with labor on an equal footing." Rogers agrees that a basic income helps protect the worker, but insists on the need for a powerful regulatory state and thinks it is critical to preserve and enhance arrangements such as minimum wage and collective bargaining rights. One might speculate about the "real-libertarian" legitimacy of various constraints on the labor market when an unconditional income is in place at the highest sustainable level. But as we explain in our book, all real-life basic income proposals are fully consistent with minimum wage legislation and active trade unions. There are, however, a number of trends—such as the shrinking of firm size or the expansion of part-time work and self-employment—that reduce the effectiveness of these traditional ways of correcting the balance of power in capitalist societies, and therefore increase the importance of empowering workers with a wider set of options, outside *and* inside the labor market, which is what a basic income does.

Beyond some minimal conditions, such as a safe work site, it is very difficult for labor market regulators—whether legislators, bureaucrats, or experts—to distinguish good and bad jobs. There are so many crucial factors that are very hard for them to track: the quality of the relationship between workers and their bosses and colleagues; how much the job enables workers to learn and improve their prospects; whether new technology is used to reduce discretion rather than facilitate work; how convenient the job is in terms of location and schedule; and how close the job is to the great passion of a worker's life. The workers themselves are best placed to assess these various dimensions and an unconditional basic income gives them the power to give up more easily a lousy job and accept more easily a job that may pay little or irregularly but possesses redeeming features. For this reason, it can be argued that a basic income would not only help accommodate but also encourage the growth of precarious jobs, but not of just any precarious job. A basic income empowers those who possess the relevant information, namely the workers themselves, who tend to know far more than anyone else both about the jobs concerned and about their own situations, capacities, and ambitions.

Being closer to the shop floor than labor market regulators, collective bargaining can, to some extent, achieve the same result. But basic income has the advantage of being more egalitarian. Collective bargaining improves the situation of workers in proportion to the economic value of their skills; to how much they participate in the formal labor market; to how easily their firm lends itself to unionization; and to how much nuisance capacity they possess through strikes or other means. The more "universalist" a labor organization is, and the closer one gets to "social bargaining"—with which I share Rogers's sympathy—the more this assertion needs to be qualified. The less broad a union is and the more corporatist its ideology, the more strongly it holds. By contrast, a basic income makes the biggest difference to workers most disadvantaged along the various dimensions mentioned.

Of course, the actual monetary value of the basic income matters. But even a basic income that amounts to less than the current level of means-tested social assistance for people living alone would make a significant difference. At that level, the right to conditional benefits over and above the basic income would need to be kept, so as to prevent poor households from becoming worse off. But the secure access to a modest income that can be relied upon even if one gives up a job voluntarily and that can be combined with other income would broaden the options of the worst off and thus increase their power. Such a modest basic income could not eradicate poverty on its own. But it would be more than the "baby step" discussed by Rogers, namely a basic income for parents or a universal child benefit of a sort that already exists in a number of countries. And it would be more reasonable than a bold jump to a basic income of 2,500 Swiss francs, a scheme supported by nearly a quarter of Swiss voters in their June 2016 referendum.

Like the two older forms of social protection—social assistance and social insurance—basic income will only be introduced in sustainable fashion in democratic societies if it manages to get enough support from both the left and the right. In Switzerland only the Green Party recommended voting in favor of basic income in the referendum. In Finland a right-of-center government launched a two-year basic income experiment in January 2017. In France basic income moved center stage because it was the most widely discussed component in the program of Benoit Hamon, the most left-wing candidate in the socialist party's January 2017 presidential primary. And when the European Parliament examined a resolution stating that "in the light of the possible effects on the labour market of robotics and artificial intelligence a general basic income should be seriously considered," a strong minority of 286 members (against 328) drawn from a wide variety of parties endorsed it. All of this suggests that basic income now enjoys an unprecedented level of support across the political spectrum. Not enough to guarantee that the balance of democratic power will soon make it reality. But enough to make it reasonable to hope that it will.

# Redistributing Wealth and Power

*Connie Razza*

OVER THE PAST EIGHTEEN MONTHS, in my recent capacity as Director of Campaigns at the Center for Popular Democracy, I have had many conversations with organizers and leaders at base-building organizations in black and Latino working-class communities. They have been exploring various policies that will enable the members of their communities to find employment that provides family-sustaining income, require employers to respect their workers' rights, and require that corporations contribute their fair share to the communities in which they operate. In short, these organizations are working to rebalance power.

Basic income has been a part of these conversations because of the possibility that such a cash grant system could help address changes in the structure of work, increase economic and racial equality, and compel corporations to share their wealth. Indeed basic income could function for lower-income people as wealth-generated income functions for the wealthy: a regular source of income not tied to work. However, as Brishen Rogers cautions, such outcomes are far from certain. Further, for black and Latino working-class communities, they may not be sufficient.

For a basic income to work for working-class communities and communities of color, which have long had disproportionately little power, it needs to redistribute wealth *and* power. It needs to exist next to investment in public sector jobs; be part of a robust safety net that can better address the structural racism that compounds disadvantage over time; include policy protections to ensure that the cash stays with the recipients and does not simply pass through to lenders and providers of key services and goods; and ensure that public investments that profit private enterprises generate returns for the public. Advocates must not only institute basic income, but also restructure power for working-class communities and communities of color.

AT ITS ROOT, BASIC INCOME AIMS to respond to the changing structure of the economy and labor market—the precarity of paid work, stagnant wages, uncertain hours, and the decline of workers' formal and informal bargaining power—as corporate economic and political power has grown.

As Andy Stern and others argue, basic income could serve to increase workers' bargaining power because the guaranteed cash would enable them to refuse unreasonable working conditions. However, as Rogers suggests, regulations protecting worker rights and standards would still be necessary to ensure that basic income does not function as a subsidy to employers, enabling them to reduce the employer-provided remuneration because everyone has a cushion.

Furthermore, basic income does not necessarily address some of the most tenacious and pernicious rules of our labor market. Algernon Austin has shown that, for more than a half-century, African American unemployment rates have been roughly twice as high as white unemployment rates. Structural racism—both within the labor market and in education, housing, and other related areas—largely accounts for this disparity. In addition many African Americans are trapped outside of the labor force altogether. (While many reasons for being outside the labor force are borne by different racial and ethnic groups equally, one—mass incarceration and discrimination against people with criminal records—disproportionately impacts African Americans.)

Indeed Rogers's call for a "revamped public sector" is a vital corollary to basic income. As Steven Pitts has demonstrated, the public sector has been "the single most important source of employment for African Americans." Public policy designed to overcome the history of structural racism and discrimination can be put into action through public sector employment practices. And, while some fret or fantasize about the "death of work," much of the work required for the public good—building and repairing physical infrastructure (e.g., transit and transportation, energy, water), tending to the social infrastructure (e.g., caregiving, emergency response, educating) of communities—needs doing.

BASIC INCOME ALSO AIMS to change the bedrock rules of our economy; it divorces income from work and distributes resources to people because they *are*, rather than because they work.

Proposals vary. For instance, Peter Barnes proposes a small dividend (in the range of $5,000 annually) paid to everyone for the private use (by corporations especially) of our common resources (natural and "socially created"). Andy Stern proposes an income sufficient to subsist on. Some, including Rogers, see basic income as part of the existing social safety net, while others—such as Charles Murray and Matt Zwolinski—propose that a basic income could replace the existing safety net entirely. But this latter option would be especially disastrous for the most vulnerable among us. Rogers astutely warns that any basic income design premised on rolling back the social welfare apparatus or worker protections would lead to a dystopic future.

The current social safety net targets disadvantaged recipient groups (primarily by income) in order to assure them access to necessary, quality goods and services (e.g., housing, education, health care, transportation). These existing programs put resources into the hands of individuals who need them and encourage the market to serve them, offering a modest reparation for policies and practices that have long disadvantaged people of color and with low incomes and wealth. While designs for basic income usually are structured to be progressive and benefit low-income and low-wealth people more, none ensures access to the goods and services people need.

In fact, without policy controls, basic income could exacerbate inequalities by driving inflation for necessities such as housing, childcare, and food as suppliers adapt to the baseline resources available to customers and clients. In such a scenario, the resources intended to liberate people at the lower end of the income and wealth spectrum would simply flow through to the already wealthy and powerful, disproportionately harming people of color and low-income people. Similarly, without a plan for programmatically addressing existing debt, basic income will have limited benefit for borrowers, who may end up simply signing over their basic income to their lenders.

FINALLY, THE MOST EXCITING basic income proposals aim to excavate the public contributions to private wealth generation and reap dividends for the public. "Auto manufacturers did not discover electricity," Rogers says, "and Silicon Valley did not invent the Internet." As a result this model might tax private corporations that use publicly funded research or resources and thus infuse the economy with a share of their gains. But even under this model, a basic income does not necessarily unwind corporate power.

President Donald Trump and congressional Republicans have made clear that they intend to restructure our social safety net and starve those programs; to undercut workers' rights to safe workplaces, fair compensation, and free association in unions; to move public goods and services into private control; and to champion the interests of wealthy corporations and individuals.

In the face of this effort to further concentrate wealth and power into the hands of a few, the question of the redistribution of power is vital. And it is the point at which the uneasy alliances among basic income advocates fracture. Basic income designed as a salve for masses of workers displaced by automation will only redistribute wealth but not power. Those who aim to create a more egalitarian society must envision a program that redistributes power as well.

# The Silicon Valley Case

*Roy Bahat*

FOR A LIVING, I WONDER about and try to bring about the future: I invest in technology startups—many related to artificial intelligence—that (if they succeed) will deliver a more automated world. Our firm, together with New America, has also been conducting a national scenario planning exercise to understand the 10- to 20-year outlook for work in the United States.

All this future-looking has taught me that every future hope or worry hides in the present. While Brishen Rogers argues that "reports of the death of work have been greatly exaggerated," I would argue we are feeling technology's dislocations in our joints now.

Work today is gasping for breath: labor force participation by men ages 25–54 has fallen 10 percent from a peak of 98 percent in the 1950s. Official measures of unemployment understate the severity of today's crisis by not including those who have given up trying to find work.

Rogers says that significant unemployment caused by technology has yet to materialize, but significant job loss has already followed from automation. Just look at the example of longshoremen as documented in the new podcast *Containers*.

Meanwhile a great deal of work valued by our society is poorly paid, such as eldercare, childcare, and teaching. In all, the present state of work in America is a mess. That is why we are considering proposals as sweeping as basic income.

THERE ARE MANY MISTAKEN IDEAS of what a basic income might solve. Some people believe it would solve inequality but, all other things being equal, it would barely trim the edges of the wealth gap. Others believe it would solve poverty. If poverty were only a matter of money in the bank, that might be true.

Rogers emphasizes the moral economy of work, saying, "we need a vision of good work." Put plainly, a basic income might fill our wallets while it fails to fill our days. It will fail to provide for goods that both the public sector and private markets struggle to provide, such as health care, education, and housing. It will fail to balance power.

But what power must we balance? The power of the firm? It is unclear whether, in the future, firms will be more or less powerful on average than today. In fact, while the biggest firms are getting bigger, the average size of firms is falling (as is the rate of new firm formation). It is unclear whether the power of all firms is a problem worth solving —or if it is simply a problem of those firms that are monopsonies or otherwise distortive of markets.

The long-term employment relationship between a firm and an employee has carried so much of society's load: the purpose of a job for an individual, the stability of an income for a family, health benefits, even camaraderie. Whether that relationship is fraying is also unclear.

So the need for stronger collective bargaining seems unclear—other than the form of collective bargaining we see now, in our very biggest collective, which is citizen influence on the government.

What is clear is that the typical American no longer has a fair shot at providing for an ordinary life. Many people would like to work more, if only predictable work with fair wages were available, but for the first time on record, the rich now spend more time working than the poor. Many are afraid they will be unable to provide for their loved ones and almost half would be unable to pay an unexpected expense of $400. That fear might be provoking extreme behavior (including tolerance of white nationalism). Our hunger for stability is innate.

The biggest ill a basic income might heal is fear.

With a basic income, a spouse can leave a domestic abuse situation. With a basic income, a writer might write, an actor might act, and our culture might reflect the breadth of our peoples' lived experiences. With a basic income, an entrepreneur might put a few dollars into opening a family business.

And, with a basic income, yes, some might use more opioids. But for every person who does that, many more will make their families proud.

Going forward, many professions will require a degree of personal motivation much greater than the "show up and do the job" seats many fill today. Work is noble when it is necessary.

So in addition to raising the economic floor with a basic income or an alternative to it, we need to promote the skills and mindset needed for anyone to become (if she or he chooses) a "firm of one." Self-employment would provide an alternative to employment at a big firm, and as the costs of doing business fall in many industries, the "firm of one" becomes more economically productive. It also seems clear that our society will continue to need many forms of work for which there is no payer willing to provide an ordinary life for the paid.

MANY TOWERING QUESTIONS REMAIN. How do we reconcile a basic income with American values of earning one's way? Can we create a multicultural, inclusive society that also treats its least well off with generosity? Can we sell all this politically? How should we pay for it? What government benefits might it replace? How should we design it? Is basic income like ice cream, where it will be good in any flavor? Or like mushrooms, where the difference between one variety and another is life and death?

But the conversation is happening now. If we do raise the economic floor in America, it will likely take decades to agree on a new way. In the coming years work will shift. Our families may hold together differently. Our politics might take a ninety-degree turn. We need to honor those who do necessary work for which they are unpaid or underpaid. We struggle to predict the future, so we must prepare for it and address the crisis we already face today.

# A New Social Contract

## *David Rolf & Corrie Watterson*

AS ECONOMISTS AND FUTURISTS DEBATE whether technology-driven unemployment is imaginable in our lifetimes, we join our labor colleague Andy Stern in calling for a basic income as part of a strategy to rebalance the scales for American workers. The labor movement's job has always been to ensure that workers get a fair slice of the economic pie. We have been winning higher minimum wages around the country, and those wins have made a real difference. But the overarching forces that are suppressing wages and transforming work are now too powerful and entrenched for our much-weakened labor movement to directly defeat.

We agree wholeheartedly with Brishen Rogers that a basic income will be necessary—but not sufficient—to build an inclusive economy in an era of mass economic disruption. The problem is not simply that wages are broadly stagnant; it is also that the balance of power between the average worker and those who are calling the shots is wildly askew. As we contemplate how to respond to the seismic changes in the economy, we cannot just aim to prevent people from starving. We need to fight for "the 99 percent" to have a hand on the wheel of the economy alongside corporations, financiers, and legislators.

A modest basic income is not a silver bullet. On its own, basic income is unlikely to provide a livable income—most of the figures that advocates are proposing are in the arena of $10,000 to $15,000 per year. That's just enough to eradicate extreme poverty and support a more stable, creative, or comfortable life for everyone else. Most people would still need to work or would strongly prefer to, at least when they can. They would still be subject to the rising costs of health care and education. Jobs would continue to offer less stability and fewer benefits, and income inequality would continue to grow. Even with a basic income, then, there would still be a pressing need to develop a new framework that includes a more comprehensive set of shared benefits for all Americans; a revised employment "contract" for the modern economy; and better vehicles for workers to exercise bargaining power.

Basic income is an example of a universal benefit administered by the government, but it is not the only one we advocate. Others include easily accessible and affordable child care, retirement, health care, long-term care for the elderly, higher education and apprenticeships, and a program of direct employment to rebuild American infrastructure and tighten labor markets. These social benefits should be financed primarily through taxes or social insurance premiums, not through employer payroll costs.

American workers also need a new deal from their employers. In addition to a minimum wage of at least fifteen dollars an hour, Americans should demand that employers abide by a minimum set of legally enforceable expectations including pay equity, paid family and medical leave, predictable scheduling, anti-discrimination protections, and a system of portable benefits for workers not covered by employer-provided plans. We must also reorient how the economic and political power of government impacts working people and push for more democratic, balanced, pro-worker stances in trade agreements, corporate governance, monetary policy, campaign finance, and criminal justice.

Underpinning our ability to win all of these reforms is worker power, which formerly was wielded by labor unions. But organized labor thrived in an era of standardized industrial production, long-term employment in an industry or firm, and the relative immobility of both workers and capital. It has long pursued a strategy that is past its expiration date. And since the 1980s, American employers have engaged in an all-out effort to destroy unions, an effort now abetted by right-wing politicians at the state level who have made it harder to form and maintain unions and limited the scope of collective bargaining. The same cohort has completely blocked progressive labor law reform at the federal level.

The most important single task left to today's remaining unions, then, is to seed innovation and discover powerful, scalable, sustainable new models of worker organization. Instead of relying on the increasingly inaccessible structures of traditional enterprise-based collective bargaining, many of the new 'alt-labor' efforts use public, legislative, and electoral pressure to improve wages and work. These models, Rogers notes, also "better reflect contemporary production relationships among firms, suppliers, and workers" than twentieth century–style unions. But almost without exception worker centers and other alt-labor formations lack the economic and political power, scale, and revenue sustainability of twentieth-century unions.

There are a number of potential overlapping strategies for how new forms of worker organizations might operate, all of which could be prototyped at the city or state level:

*Regional and sectoral bargaining over minimum standards*
Standards for wages and benefits can be set throughout an industry or within a geographic area, negotiated by representatives of employers, workers and government. Examples include wage setting boards; the stakeholder process we used in Seattle for the fifteen dollar minimum wage negotiations in 2014; and New York's process for a fifteen dollar fast food worker wage in 2015.

*Benefits administration*
Worker organizations could replace employers as the primary providers and administrators of worker benefits that are universal, portable, and prorated. Workers would earn and accrue benefits on a per-hour basis into a portable account. Examples are New York's Black Car Fund and legislation introduced in Washington State this year to create a portable benefits system.

*Labor standards enforcement*
Worker organizations could begin to "represent" workers through onsite enforcement of labor standards and employment laws, either within a geographic area or an industry. Examples include the Coalition of Immokalee Workers (the farm workers that Rogers references), the Workers Defense Project (Austin construction-industry employees), and SEIU's Maintenance Cooperation Trust Fund (California).

*Certification & labeling*
Companies could earn a label or certification by registering with a worker-led nonprofit organization, adhering to certain labor and employment standards, and agreeing to audits by the certifying organization. Successful examples include the Fair Trade label and LEED conservation standards.

*Codetermination*

In parts of Europe, labor agreements are made at the national level by unions and employer associations, and firms meet with "works councils" to adjust the agreements to local circumstances. Workers at German companies elect a council to resolve workplace issues, and large companies are required to have worker representation on their boards; in the United States, a variation is used by health care company Kaiser Permanente.

*Worker ownership*

Employees earn or purchase an equity stake in their companies, gaining direct control over the selection of a management team, reinvestment in the firm, and compensation. A successful U.S. example is Cooperative Home Care Associates in the Bronx. Employee stock purchase plans, or ESOPs, accomplish some of the same goals as worker-owned firms and are much more common.

*Advocacy*

Membership-based advocacy organizations such as AARP, Planned Parenthood, the NRA, the ACLU, Greenpeace, and MoveOn have achieved significant and ongoing political power. The largest of these organizations are "functional" rather than just "issue" oriented, as Peter Murray notes in "The Secret of Scale" (2013). Groups such as the AARP (various insurance products) and the NRA (gun safety insurance) offer benefits or services that are purchased not because it is the right thing to do, but because they are "relevant to the daily lives" of members.

*Job training and placement*

Worker organizations could partner with schools, employers, and government to promote skill development and job placement. Examples include the SEIU Healthcare Northwest Training Partnership in

Washington State, which trains three thousand home-care aides a year, and the Registered Apprenticeship College Consortium, a partnership among community colleges, national accreditors, employers, and major apprenticeship sponsors.

IT IS DIFFICULT TO FATHOM a basic income policy standing alone in an environment that is hostile to inclusive prosperity, to broadly sharing the economic gains made possible by technology. But with powerful worker organizations we can, in Rogers's words, "reduce elites' domination of our politics, which may otherwise prevent implementation of a basic income, limit its generosity, or set it up to fail." Indeed it may be that the "union 2.0" project needs to come first to see it across the finish line—and protect it once it is in place.

Basic income proponents from the tech sector, nonprofits, academia, and labor must ally and craft a compact that incorporates both strategies, to be developed in tandem: basic income to provide an income floor, and independent new institutions that can influence wages and working conditions. The economic security provided by a basic income program would then work in concert with other social programs, legal changes, and innovations in worker bargaining.

If we are not successful, the same forces that led us to this moment will continue to rule us. And the longer it goes on, the closer we slouch toward a dystopian future of an advanced technological culture, one which could have been a dream of prosperity but instead is used to entrench the rule of the few over the many. Basic income is a ray of sunshine in that dark vision, pointing the way toward a shared economic future that feels both hopeful and possible.

# The Limits of Basic Income

*Brishen Rogers*

AMONG THE THOUGHTFUL AND GENEROUS RESPONSES to my essay, there is a recurring objection to my argument that we should be clear about the limits of basic income.

I recognize that few academics, activists, or commentators view basic income as the sole reform needed for economic justice, and I did not mean to suggest otherwise. I did mean to suggest that the net effects of any basic income would depend on its institutional design and on surrounding policies and institutions—especially labor and employment laws, in-kind public benefits, and the state's role as an employer. And I did mean to suggest that those surrounding policies and their effects on corporate power and workers' lack of power have not received enough attention in either the popular basic income debate or the broader debate around the future of work.

This is especially true in and around Silicon Valley. Roy Bahat is right to emphasize that our old regulations of work are not as helpful anymore—but then why not change them? I have not seen a single quote from a tech leader or thinker to the effect that "basic income is a great idea, but we also need a high minimum wage and much stronger unions." In fact, while I was drafting this response, *Harvard Business Review* published a piece tracing how information technologies have exacerbated income inequality by encouraging outsourcing and the growth of new mega-firms. But its proposal to help low-wage workers is through a negative income tax; it never once mentions minimum wages or collective bargaining.

Similarly, while I agree with most of Philippe van Parijs's nuanced response, I disagree in part with its assessment of the problems of work. For example, workers choosing between jobs do not necessarily "possess the relevant information" about those jobs' prospects and conditions, as van Parijs attests. The new management techniques I surveyed suggest that workers actually have less unique information about jobs these days, particularly—as Annette Bernhardt points out—when online labor platforms forbid them from communicating with one another.

Who does have such information? Google, Uber, Amazon, Walmart, and other mega-firms inside and outside the tech sector. A basic income would not close this knowledge gap, nor would it make it significantly easier for workers to close it through deliberation, since that requires concerted action that is difficult under current law. In fact, I worry that this knowledge gap simply cannot be closed. Data analytics are too advanced. Protecting workers may require more heavy-handed regulation, and what Joshua Cohen and Joel Rogers have called a "deliberate politics of association," in which the state positively encourages unions and organizations as sites of countervailing power.

There are of course valid reasons to embrace tax-based strategies rather than regulatory ones: concern for the unemployed, skepticism that unions can ever reorganize, and the fact that the U.S. model of unionization, as van Parijs rightly observes, tends to help certain workers more than others in morally arbitrary ways. Plus only a fool would expect the business community in the United States to enthusiastically back labor's cause.

But—and this is a key point—the law does not just regulate economic activity. It also enables and shapes economic activity in the first instance. As we evolve from industrial capitalism toward informational capitalism, ever-smaller workplaces, part-time work, and self-employment are not inevitable. Rather they reflect firms' responses to legal rules. Legislatures and courts have chosen to limit firms' employment duties and unions' powers to strike, which encourages outsourcing and other sorts of precarious work. As Diane Coyle points out, Uber drivers do much better in some legal environments than in others.

In a culture in which these political-economic effects of law are largely ignored, Silicon Valley's enthusiasm for basic income is having some detrimental effects on the ground. When foundations and think tanks flood the zone with research into the "Future of Work" (now a genre of its own), research into the realities of work today can go unfunded. That has happened to some of my colleagues. Similarly, as it becomes common sense that workers' largest challenge is automation, basic labor standards and worker organizing seem futile since higher wages will just hasten the robots' arrival. This is a false choice. I agree strongly with Coyle and Bernhardt that those concerned about inequality should embrace technological development and steer its path.

I even hold out hope that at least some in Silicon Valley could move toward this agenda, or accommodate it if they must. Flexicurity is, after all, still capitalist. Danish employers can hire and fire workers at will, just as they can in the United States, and the country embraces free trade and innovation. It even just appointed an ambassador to the tech sector. And while Danish unions are quite powerful, they do not typically bargain over work rules, but rather set high minimum standards and then leave firms free to manage. If part of Silicon Valley's skepticism toward unions is a function of peculiarities of U.S. labor law, more awareness of alternative labor law models might change things.

In other words, I would love it if "Flexicurity Bros" became the new "Basic Income Bros."

For now, though, am I really mistaken that some proponents' love for basic income leads them to overestimate its promise? Juliana Bidadanure ends her essay by arguing that basic income "has an unequalled potential to foster convergence" between otherwise atomized groups and individuals, and to "be the cornerstone of a powerful alternative progressive imaginary." Not "a" cornerstone but "the" cornerstone—the foundation upon which other ideas must build.

Dorian Warren ends up in a similar position, drawing from black political traditions and the racial capitalism literature to argue that U+BI could be the centerpiece of a multiracial campaign for economic justice. I fully agree that race neutrality is not a means to economic or racial justice, especially in the United States. But I chose many of those policies specifically because their effects would not be race-neutral. A job guarantee, heavy investment in local infrastructure, expansion of social insurance, and social bargaining for low-wage workers would disproportionately benefit African Americans and Latinos, not to mention poor and working-class women.

In fact, my ultimate narrow defense of a basic income—or perhaps a "base" income, in Peter Barnes's terms—is rooted in my hope that it could help us move past our racialized approach to welfare, which Tommie Shelby and Connie Razza also illuminate and condemn. On a related note, Bidadanure and Warren both rightly argue that the threat of a xenophobic basic income is a reason to resist xenophobia, not to abandon basic income.

To be clear, I agree fully with Bidadanure—and Warren, van Parijs, and many others—that "everyone should have an unconditional right to be free from basic economic insecurity." I just disagree that organizing around basic income is obviously the best strategy to advance that goal in the United States.

Why? First, because a basic income cannot substitute for social insurance, and social insurance remains meager in the United States. Lack of health care, housing, childcare, and mental health services leaves millions economically insecure. Providing those goods to all citizens or residents will also create jobs and perhaps a more highly skilled workforce. In fact, passing a basic income without sound social insurance programs may do more harm than good. The situation is of course different in many European countries.

Second, and at the risk of sounding like a broken record, we cannot hope to pass an egalitarian basic income in the United States without changing the power structure. Which of the following seems more plausible: that a multiracial movement of the poor and precarious will make common cause with tech billionaires to pass an egalitarian basic income; or that a multiracial movement of the poor, precarious, and middle class will push for and achieve better health care, childcare, education, and wage per hour laws? Then take on harder fights, for a new collective bargaining model, a public jobs guarantee, and cash benefits for parents? And then still harder fights, such as a generous basic income?

History does not repeat itself, but it does rhyme. If progressive politics has a new imaginary, it is an iteration of the old imaginary that made capitalism relatively fair in the postwar period: social democracy. Or, more precisely but less succinctly: racially egalitarian, feminist, and ecologically sustainable social democracy. Such a model would have many cornerstones, including economic security, worker empowerment, fair equality of opportunity, reproductive rights, an end to mass incarceration, meaningful opportunities for democratic engagement, and a real strategy on climate change.

Sometimes those goals will be in tension. Sometimes the change agents—new unions and citizen organizations—will need to be built from scratch, generally through battles to pass reforms. But unlike basic income, majorities intuitively support most of these goals—they are rooted in our political traditions, and they directly address power disparities, as Patrick Diamond, David Rolf, and Corrie Watterson show. Pushing them will alienate some libertarians, but that is politics. And doing so may enable different political coalitions, for example with religious voters committed to economic and social equality.

None of this means we should abandon basic income research or organizing, or that we should give up on steps toward it. These include universal child credits, elder credits, and even state-level efforts in places such as California, where labor and the left are already strong. But it does mean we should, as I wrote, "be clear-eyed about the policy's justifications, merits, and limits." That, in my view, is the path to economic security for all.

# A Jobless Utopia

*David McDermott Hughes*

IN 1905 THE SPANISH WRITER Vivente Blasco Ibáñez described the horrible conditions of day laborers in the vineyards outside Jerez. Barely paid, almost starving, and sleeping on hay, the day laborers in Blasco Ibáñez's novel, *La Bodega*, stumble through life as "cadavers, with twisted spines and dry limbs, deformed and clumsy."

But Blasco Ibáñez—a sort of Dickens of Andalusia—imagines a different fate for his protagonist. Our hero escapes with his fiancée to South America, "that young world" where land ownership is not a prerequisite for a good life. "What an Eden," the narrator interjects, "so much better for the eager and strong peasant, a slave until then in body and soul to those who do not work." The lovers "would be new, innocent, and industrious." The novel ends happily—there is no doubt of that—but on a mixed metaphor, with an Eden where people work hard. Indeed Blasco Ibáñez's term for "industrious"—*laborioso*—also translates as "toilsome."

What sort of Eden is this, where women and men till the soil? In Genesis, Adam and Eve simply pick fruit from orchards in perpetual bloom. At the Fall, God invents work as punishment and commands his children, "You shall gain your bread by the sweat of your own brow." Blasco, however, views a certain form of labor as a reward, and most social critics have shared this perspective. Like most myths, Eden tolerates ambiguity.

Now reformers everywhere may have to resolve the dilemma of toilsome versus leisurely Edens. Much of the world is approaching what Jeremy Rifken calls "the end of work" and, more recently, "the zero marginal cost society." In a zero marginal cost society, machines and computer algorithms replace virtually all human effort in the production of good and services.

Rural Andalusia never had much retail, but its interior villages used to grow a variety of crops under the laborious conditions described by Blasco Ibáñez. In the last two decades, however, an almost effortless form of green energy has moved in. Wind turbines now crowd the terrain and there are few jobs, agricultural or otherwise. As an anthropologist, I began visiting a village familiar with these machines, hoping to see how people live with unemployment within a landscape that has been transformed from fields into electrical infrastructure.

IN THE TINY, FOUR-HUNDRED-PERSON SETTLEMENT of La Zarzuela, spindly poles rise up ninety meters to loom over fields exotically—menacingly to some. With a smooth efficiency, sixty-meter blades propel current to people far away. The energy is clean in every sense. Once constructed and erected, a turbine consumes no raw materials. It produces no pollution. It also requires next to no maintenance.

"They are robots," boasted the manager of the largest wind farm. Indeed the company that owns that farm—the Spanish firm Acciona—is so confident in automation that it does not even have a twenty-four-hour control room on site. Instead screens in Mexico monitor La Zarzuela's farm alongside hundreds of wind farms worldwide.

Meanwhile unemployed men of a certain age cluster at two bars. Supported by Spain's social safety net, they think only sporadically about finding work. These men endured hard labor in their youth, but no one wants to return to that now. When machinery replaced the hoe and sickle, day laborers learned to drive tractors, a modest technology more like a motorcycle than a robot. But turbines upset that balance between device and operator, effectively dispensing with the latter, and as my drinking mates see it, turbines are jobs gone missing.

In a way clean energy is too clean, too divorced from the people and social context around it. Proponents of wind power—and I count myself in this group—will succeed or fail based on our ability to solve this problem. What should the balance of work and leisure be after fossil fuels? How should we imagine utopia?

LA ZARZUELA HUDDLES IN A VALLEY just north of the Straits of Gibraltar. There the pressure gradient between marine and terrestrial zones stimulates constant wind. Extending inland, two ridges frame the village in a V. They often funnel the strong, east wind, *el Levante*, into a howling squall. It has scoured the vegetation down to scrub bushes, the indigenous *acebuche*, and locals do not bother to plant trees, except for palms. *El Levante* creates the perfect conditions for wind power. Construction of wind farms began in 1999 and proceeded in spates.

When I arrived in mid-2015, almost 250 turbines were clustered within a roughly 3-by-6-mile strip. Three companies own the farms, which are called *parques eolicos*, since the notion of a wind "park" is meant to calm concern. But protests have dogged the turbines in La Zarzuela and in many other places as well. People object to the visual impact, the constant noise, and the strobe-like shadows cast in various times and seasons. In 2006 and 2007, as the government authorized another expansion, residents of La Zarzuela rallied against the "*masificacion de molinos*" (the massing of the windmills). They blocked a road, preventing construction equipment from reaching the site, rallied at the municipal town hall in Tarifa, and then lost. Big Wind—as critics term Acciona and similarly sized firms—almost always wins.

At the El Pollo bar, I found men still nursing a grudge.

"I am annoyed," declared La Zarzuela's mayor, a short stocky man known for blunt talk. Osvaldo Santiago (a pseudonym, as are all the names below) works as a foreman in the port of Algeciras, just across a narrow bay from Gibraltar itself.

"*Nadie! Nadie!*" he says while jabbing at my stomach. "No one, no one" has gotten a job from these monstrous blades. Local unemployment is 40 percent, he tells me. The turbines only require a few maintenance workers—educated, skilled technicians of the sort you won't find in rural Andalusia. Santiago, who hangs out with the captains and deck hands of container ships, cannot quite believe that such large hunks of steel can run themselves.

We can expect more such conflict and resentment. Denmark generates roughly 40 percent of its electricity from wind; Spain follows at roughly 20 percent. For now proponents and opponents agree on one tacit principle: that turbines should stay out of the way and preferably out of sight. Installers run them along ridges, in the empty spaces between settlement, or out at sea. But even this last option can provoke staunch resistance. Well-connected residents of Hyannis, Massachusetts, all but killed the 130-turbine Cape Wind project in the 2000s because they contended it would "pollute" their ocean views. Americans seem to prefer their windmills in Iowa, west Texas, and eastern Oregon, hinterlands where few people (and fewer rich people) live and vote. Unfortunately much of that electricity dies on the cables, never reaching refrigerators and light bulbs hundreds of miles away. Therein lies the problem: to power the grid with 100 percent renewables, every society will need to put wind farms and solar farms in places where the wind blows, where the sun shines, and where consumers of electricity live. Saving the planet from catastrophic climate change is going to be inconvenient.

Oil has been quite convenient, especially in terms of space. A hole in the ground less than three feet across can provide enough fuel to power a city. Even if one adds up all the infrastructure of rigs, pipelines, refineries, and gas stations, petroleum occupies very little land. Compare that modest footprint with the forests of colonial New England that were once obliterated to heat and light Boston. Those trees have returned, thanks to fossil fuels, and every Appalachian hiker benefits from that spatial subsidy (in addition to the gasoline that brings her to the trailhead). By refining compact kernels of hydrocarbon power, Americans liberated landscapes from servitude as fuel. Now, with great reluctance, we will have to reconsider this deal. Given that the arrangement will eventually cost us New Orleans, Miami, Boston, and New York, we clearly did not strike such a good bargain after all.

La Zarzuela provides a test case for a new deal between energy and landscapes. Against the will of the people, Big Wind converted field and pasture into an energy platform. The cost in acres was not immediately apparent; landowners still run cattle and plant crops around the turbines. But interior Andalusia had only recently begun attracting tourists, a promising new economic opportunity that the wind industry effectively squashed.

Alejandro Baptista knows about this defeat firsthand. His family owns the Doña Lola Hotel, a coastal resort, as well as the two-and-a-half-mile wind strip between the Atlantic and La Zarzuela. In 2004 the municipality surveyed that strip as a "vacation city." Baptista dreamt of building holiday chalets and even a golf course, developments that would have employed the people of La Zarzuela. Tourism promised jobs and garnered local support, while the landowner stood poised to cash in.

Then turbines spoiled the vista. Baptista, who cannot imagine that a tourist would appreciate the whirring blades, opposed the turbines and joined the protest—up to the last minute, when he capitulated. Now he collects an annual rent, calibrated to the generating capacity of each of the fourteen turbines on his property. The money—approximately $2,500 per machine—falls far below what he might earn from tourism. But it vastly exceeds what any individual in La Zarzuela takes home.

Local residents believe that Baptista sold out. Big Wind cost Baptista his view and his reputation. Meanwhile turbines did nothing good for the local economy. The industrious Eden—possibly something like Blasco Ibáñez's New World utopia—slipped away.

BUT WHAT IS UTOPIA to the men of La Zarzuela? Sugar beets used to be a major crop in the village, but they are tedious and arduous to grow. As a root crop, sugar beets require men to bend at the waist, manipulating the tuber in the soil with a long-handled hoe. First workers thin the crop, cutting out three of every four roots. Those gaps allow workers to then reach the roots when, some months later, they are harvested.

At El Pollo Diego tells me that the labor was "*insoportable*" and "*durísima*" (unbearable and hard). In the ninety-degree heat of summer, day laborers would load sugar beets directly onto trucks all day long.

Using my pen and notebook, Diego does some calculations. Each truck would carry 20,000 kilograms, and a team of eight could fill two trucks, meaning each laborer would harvest 5,000 kilograms (or 11,000 pounds) per day. It sounds like a Herculean feat to me, and Diego looks me in the eye to convince me that he is not exaggerating. Next to him another veteran of the beet harvest runs fingers down his face, mimicking perspiration.

Still in disbelief at such a hellish outdoor sweatshop, I check with Baptista, who grew sugar beets from 1975 to 2009, long after other growers had given up. I expect him to understate the drudgery he imposed on day laborers, but instead he warms to the topic. Day laborers loaded and cleaned the beets at a pay rate of 1.10 peseta (about a penny) per kilogram. I get confused, thinking he has said 100 pesetas per kilogram. No, Baptista laughs gleefully, 1,100 pesetas *per* ton.

"Loaded *and* cleaned," he repeats with enthusiasm.

When La Zarzuela's men refused to break their backs in this way any longer, migrant laborers from Granada took over the harvest. Eventually the crop shifted to northern Spain, where it grows more economically, under irrigation and mechanical harvesting, and the Baptistas moved on to other crops, to hotels, and, of course, to turbines.

With little sadness, hard labor in La Zarzuela went extinct, but there is still nostalgia for less onerous forms of labor. In the Gazquez bar, just up the road from El Pollo, painted tiles show men cutting wheat with sickles and women carrying it away, and the barroom's conversations about grain differ in tone from those about beets. A man named Jaime smiles, recalling how horses trampled the harvest. Men would then toss it in the air using pitchforks while women carried out drinks to them. This harvest brought families and neighbors together. Old men crowd around Jaime and me, describing their personal experiences, while those middle-aged or younger recall stories from their parents.

Mateo explains that one winnowed wheat when *el Poniente*—the weaker, westerly wind—was blowing. Stronger gusts would have blown away the kernels with the chaff.

Although this work also took place in summer, no one recalls the heat or any sense of oppressive toil. No one mentions teams of workers, tonnages, or piecework, although I am speaking to the same men who had also handled beets. These men, mostly in their seventies, know a kind of work that adds to human dignity, family bonds, and the spirit of community. Pepe pays for my drink as he leaves, evidently pleased with our chat.

Hand winnowing ended in the 1960s with the arrival of a fixed threshing machine. Then, from 1975 onwards, combine harvesters took over. On the surface, wheat went the way of sugar beets, but no one in La Zarzuela sees them as parallels. Winnowing began as a task and became an expression of social life and environmental knowledge. It must have been arduous work sometimes, but not all the time. The painter of Gazguez's tiles, for instance, overlooked the sweat on the brows of the men cutting and tossing grain. Between utter toil and joblessness lies this remembered Eden of labor. Can people in La Zarzuela fight their way—past combines and turbines—back to that utopia? Should they?

WIND FARMS APPEAR MORE RESTFUL than industrious. Workers do not surround the turbine or coax it to spin as do, say, drillers on an oil rig. Proponents argue that the expansion of the wind industry will generate hundreds of thousands of green jobs in the United States alone—far more than are now found in coal—as electricians, crane operators, and so on still have to install any given turbine. The "clean energy revolution" will bring a construction boom lasting a decade or two, they argue. But then the turbines will virtually run themselves.

Clean energy is structured that way. Karl Marx, who knew nothing about turbines, described labor as "a process by which man, through his own actions, mediates, regulates, and controls the metabolism between himself and nature." That metabolism converts raw materials into products and, also, into waste. Miners, for instance, extract iron ore from the ground; further work is required to refine it into workable metal and still more to manage the discarded rock.

A turbine is utterly different. Its raw material—if one can even call it that—blows downwind. No one needs to dig for the breeze. Kinetically-charged air simply arrives and turns the blades, and electricity flows to the grid. There is no product to carry and certainly no pollution to cart off, bury, or otherwise handle. The dirt, the dust, the pile, the load—the physical signs by which we know the dignity of labor—are all missing here. Where is the work?

With some effort on my own part, I find technicians around La Zarzuela. After driving my rental car through the wind farms, ignoring the warnings that say "Authorized Personnel Only," I encounter Ramiro, a ruddy, bearded man in his fifties dressed in a blue uniform. He and his partner are sitting in their truck at the top of a rise, enjoying the view of La Zarzuela and the sea. I ask him about his job. It is great, he tells me. They pay whether he has to do anything or not—much better than working with "*pico y pala*," pick and shovel. He also enthuses about nature, the view, and the tranquility of his wind farm. We chat for half an hour as blades swoosh gracefully around us. Then he drives off for his lunch break.

A few days later, I meet up with another technician named Jorge in Tarifa, the larger municipality to which La Zarzuela belongs. Jorge is active on social media, posting photos he takes of the turbines as well as photos of the view taken from atop them. He drives a black BMW, which I follow as he takes me to the beach outside town. We lean on the hood of his car, framed by waves on the west and bladed hillsides to the east. Jorge—who likes his job at least as much as Ramiro does—works on contract doing the infrequent refurbishing of the turbines. He is now fielding inquiries from as far away as Chile. Twenty-six years old and handsome, Jorge likens himself to a soccer player resting between global tours. Friends drive by and wave as he talks about nature, each of us gazing up at the turbines along the ridges.

Meanwhile electricity is surging from those turbines. On one of the arrays outside La Zarzuela, twenty machines generate two megawatts of electricity each. Only five technicians service those turbines, which means each worker produces eight megawatts of energy—with time leftover to shoot photos and take in the scenery. In the blow-zone of the straits, technology is enabling a lifestyle of relaxation, enjoyment, and beauty. Some might even call it a utopia.

TO LIVE COMFORTABLY WITH WIND POWER, we will have to set aside deep-rooted biases. From Marx to Blasco Ibáñez to Barack Obama, observers of society have hewed to what Max Weber called the Protestant Work Ethic: one should toil industriously, make a product, and enjoy the fruits of that labor. Leisure must be earned. Perhaps because of Eve's trespass, readers of the Bible feel they do not automatically deserve idleness or even hobbies. Labor gives us identity and, when it is good labor, the dignity and self-worth of a person fulfilled.

Some have dissented. In 1883 the Cuban-born writer Paul Lafargue advocated a "right to be lazy." Modern machines, he found, produced enough to support both those working with them and a greater population made redundant by them. Lafargue, who married Karl Marx's daughter after emigrating to London, also argued for shortening the work day. By 1930 the economist John Maynard Keynes was on board as well, predicting a machine-driven, post-work society. "Three hours a day is quite enough to satisfy the old Adam in most of us," he wrote, referring to the farmer after the Fall.

Some critics of capitalism now call for a "multi-activity society," one that supports hobbies, sports, art, political action, and caring for children and parents. My state, New Jersey, has already embarked down that road—in an ecological fashion. The electrical grid pays me for doing nothing, though the transaction is complicated. In 1999 the Board of Public Utilities established an incentive program to encourage home-owners to install solar panels. As a beneficiary of this policy, I consume free electricity equivalent to my generation, meaning that I almost never pay an electric bill. But I also sell the "environmental attributes" of that electricity, known as a Solar Renewable Energy Certificate. I earn a certificate with every zero-carbon megawatt-hour I generate, which I can then auction to power companies so that they can include it in their quota of renewables, as mandated by state law. In other words, I get electricity for free *and* I earn more than $1,000 per year from my 22 rooftop panels. That second benefit compensates me, not for work or investment, but for environmental stewardship.

That planet-saving principle is sound, but other people deserve these payments more than homeowners in New Jersey. As they lose their jobs to solar power, coal miners and plant workers are reducing carbon emissions dramatically. Under the logic that pays me, they surely deserve their own, larger share of the $400 million annual market for New Jersey solar certificates. If I get a check for raising kids under my roof on a sunny weekend, then coal country ought to claim a subsidy for its no-wage, multi-activity society.

To agree to that transfer of resources, politicians and the public have to accept a place such as La Zarzuela for what it is. Many in the United States are likely to agree with hard-driving Santiago, the mayor in La Zarzuela, who cannot bear what he sees as idleness. He would prefer that his neighbors load freight, assisted by petroleum, from port of port. One should make something or move something—or, at the very least, perform a service that others value enough to pay for. We have been taught that we earn money "by the sweat of our own brows," as God allegedly put it at the Fall. We should not, as before the Fall, simply receive bread because there is enough to go around. As long as this insistence upon production prevails, we will remain mired in a system of industry and energy completely unsuited to today's ecological conditions. Perhaps, in order to relinquish fossil fuels, we need to learn to forgive ourselves and others for not working.

At El Pollo unemployed men and women come to drink beer and coffee. They pay with welfare money or wages from last summer's tourism and they are, by and large, content. Nearby, the Caseta Municipal, the local club, offers free yoga classes for adults, soccer games for kids, and flamenco festivals for everyone. All the while massive robots do the serious, manual work. Some La Zarzuela residents might object to their appearance, but the turbines do their work without changing the climate—and to some, they even change the landscape for the better. To me, these circumstances seem as close to utopia as I could ever to expect to witness.

# The Right to Strike

*James Gray Pope, Ed Bruno, & Peter Kellman*

IN DECEMBER 2005 more than thirty thousand New York City transit workers walked out over economic issues despite the state of New York's Taylor Law, which prohibits all public sector strikes. Not only did the workers face the loss of two days' pay for each day on strike, but a court ordered that the union be fined $1 million per day. Union president Roger Toussaint held firm, likening the strikers to Rosa Parks. "There is a higher calling than the law," he declared. "That is justice and equality."

The transit strike exemplified labor civil disobedience at its most effective. The workers were not staging a symbolic event; they brought the city's transit system to a halt. They claimed their fundamental right to collective action despite a statute that outlawed it. For a precious moment, public attention was riveted on the drama of workers defying a draconian strike ban.

How did national labor leaders react?

AFL-CIO president John Sweeney issued a routine statement of support, while most others did nothing at all. To anybody watching the drama unfold, the message was clear: there is no right to strike, even in the House of Labor.

About a decade earlier in 1996, Stephen Lerner, fresh from a successful campaign to organize Los Angeles janitors, had warned in *Boston Review* that private sector unions faced an existential crisis: density could soon drop from 10.3 percent to 5 percent if unions did not expand their activity beyond the limits imposed by American law. He called for unions to develop broad organizing strategies—industry-wide and regional—and to engage in civil disobedience. Few embraced these radical strategies. Today private sector union density is about 6.5 percent, not quite as low as Lerner predicted, but down from a high of over 30 percent in the mid-1950s.

Union decline matters. For half a century, it has moved in lock step with the increase in income inequality. According to an International Monetary Fund study of twenty advanced economies, union decline accounted for about half of the increase in net income inequality from 1980 to 2012. In the heyday of American unionism, CEOs made about twenty-five times the annual compensation of the average worker; today, the multiple is more than 350. Meanwhile, as Thomas Edsell and others have warned for decades, the decline of unions has deprived the Democratic Party of its strongest link to white workers. The overwhelming majority of unions continue to endorse Democratic candidates (including Hillary Clinton in the 2016 election), but with ever-diminishing effect.

Until two decades ago it was possible to blame union decline on backward labor leaders, such as George Meany, who were so steeped in business unionism that they could not see the need to organize broadly, much less to ally with other social movements across lines of race, gender, and immigration status. Since then, however, we have seen continued shrinkage under leaders who are, for the most part, well intentioned and savvy.

The problem is structural. National union officials are not well positioned to lead a challenge to corporate power. Institutions with big treasuries and tit-for-tat relations with establishment politicians cannot be expected to undertake risky and polarizing actions. Although leaders might see the need to build working-class power, the immediate incentives all point toward the narrow needs of their particular union's members. This constraint is rooted in the American system of exclusive representation, which divides workers into thousands of bargaining unit boxes, gives unions property interests in particular boxes, and penalizes unions for doing anything other than defending existing boxes and acquiring new ones.

The prospects for union revival may seem bleaker than ever during the Trump administration, even as the triumph of right-wing populism makes more urgent what was already apparent: the need to build a labor movement that can fight for the interests of the working class in the face of corporate power.

But prospects are not as grim as they appear. Over the past decade, there has been an undeniable shift toward class politics, most visibly evidenced by Occupy Wall Street, the Bernie Sanders campaign, the Fight for Fifteen, and the rise of a Black Lives Matter movement that supports economic justice demands, including the right to organize. Building the labor movement in this period of danger and opportunity will require not only heeding Lerner's call for a strategic shift and extralegal action; labor must also reclaim the right to strike and confront the deep structural disabilities that impede unions from challenging corporate power.

AS LERNER DIAGNOSED TWENTY YEARS AGO, U.S. labor law blocks unions and workers from effective organizing and striking. Then as now, the law's protections for workers' rights amount to little more than paper guarantees, while its restrictions are downright deadly. Indeed the Committee on Freedom of Association of the International Labor Organization (ILO) has held that the United States is violating international standards by failing to protect the right to organize, by banning secondary strikes and boycotts across the board, and by allowing employers to permanently replace workers who strike. The ban on secondary strikes is especially debilitating, because it prevents workers who have economic power, such as organized grocery workers, from aiding workers who do not, for example unorganized packing house workers. If the grocery workers support striking packers by refusing to handle food packed by strikebreakers, they are said to be engaging in an illegal secondary strike.

But the law cuts even deeper, deforming workers' organizations at their inception. As amended by the Taft-Hartley Act of 1947 (tagged by unionists as the "Slave Labor Law"), the National Labor Relations Act (NLRA) confronts workers with a choice between two inadequate forms of organization: statutory "labor organizations," popularly known as unions, and "others," for example workers' centers that organize outside the statutory framework. At first glance, the choice seems obvious. Only unions can demand and engage in collective bargaining. But unions are subject to so many restrictions that some workers' organizations (such as the Restaurant Opportunities Centers United) are willing to forego collective bargaining in order to avoid them, while others (including the Coalition of Immokalee Workers) consider themselves lucky to be excluded from the NLRA altogether. In the 1960s Cesar Chavez of the United Farm Workers rejected NLRA coverage for farm workers on the ground that it would inscribe "a glowing epitaph on our tombstone."

The obvious response would be to reform the law. But labor faces a double bind: American workers have never won a significant piece of workers' rights legislation without first engaging in exactly the kind of strikes and other forms of noncooperation that current labor laws forbid. The Erdman Act of 1898, the Clayton Act of 1914, the Railway Labor Act of 1926, the Norris-LaGuardia Anti-Injunction Act of 1932, the Wagner Act (NLRA) of 1935, and the public sector collective bargaining laws of the 1970s were all preceded by dramatic strikes and mass disobedience.

By comparison, organized labor's more recent legislative campaigns all failed despite Democratic ascendancy in both houses of Congress and the White House. The Labor Law Reform bill of 1978, the striker replacement bills of the early 1990s, and the Employee Free Choice Act (EFCA) of 2007–9 succumbed to a combination of tepid presidential support (Carter, Clinton, and Obama to labor leaders: "I'm with you; just wait until I've spent my political capital on other things") and the filibuster. Even if enacted, those bills would have provided only modest protections for workers' rights, well short of the far-reaching changes necessary to reverse union decline. Given the booming influence of money on politics, the skewed representation in the Senate, and the gerrymandered House, we simply cannot expect ordinary politics to produce the reforms that would give unions a fighting chance of revival. Organizing, it seems, must precede legislation.

The Service Employees International Union (SEIU) is the only big union to launch the kind of confrontational campaign urged by Lerner. For the past four years, SEIU has poured money and organizers into the nationwide Fight for Fifteen campaign. With its combination of sectoral organizing and civil disobedience, Fight for Fifteen has scored a number of victories, including the enactment of fifteen-dollar minimum wage laws in several jurisdictions as well as the inclusion of a fifteen-dollar minimum wage plank in the Democratic Party platform. The campaign has gained SEIU few dues-paying union members—which to some critics earns it a failing grade—but it has validated organized labor as a champion of low-wage workers and accelerated the shift toward class politics.

It should come as no surprise that Fight for Fifteen has made more progress on wages than on union growth. Employers have always resisted unionization far more tenaciously than wage increases. They understand that unionism entails a workplace regime shift, while wage increases merely redistribute wealth for a time. Conversely, organized labor has never achieved major growth without prioritizing the rights to organize and strike above economic gain. The Fight for Fifteen and—for that matter—most of the labor movement's activity, would be far more effective if it were tied to a long-term strategy for winning three core rights for workers: rights to organize, strike, and act in solidarity. Lacking those rights (whether de facto or officially), the movement will be of little use in struggles for social justice or in alliances with other movements. The labor movement of the early twentieth century, which propelled unionism to its historic high, grasped this point. Even the cigar-chomping business unionists of Samuel Gompers's era seized on opportunities to trumpet the constitutional rights to organize and strike, sometimes in support of open lawbreaking by leftist unions and workers.

In order to win workers' rights, organized labor should act like a rights movement. History tells us that rights movements—from abolition to women's suffrage to civil rights—succeed when they claim a few key rights, exercise them at every opportunity, and place them front and center in every phase of movement activity, including organizing, protest, civil disobedience, legislative advocacy, administrative advocacy, and litigation. Not only does this kind of focus help to sway public opinion, but also—perhaps more importantly—it assures adherents and convinces opponents that the movement is serious. No workers contemplating extralegal exercise of labor rights should doubt that the movement will come to their support and that they are participating in a historic struggle for rights that will be carried through to victory.

How can workers claim their rights in defiance of duly enacted laws? Social movements typically answer this kind of question with reference to higher law, especially the Constitution. For example, the civil rights movement defied Jim Crow in the name of the Constitution's equal protection clause. The labor movement of the early twentieth century held that anti-strike laws established "involuntary servitude" in violation of the Thirteenth Amendment, while anti-picketing and anti-boycott laws transgressed the First Amendment freedoms of free speech and association. Neither movement waited for courts to recognize their rights; they interpreted the Constitution for themselves.

International norms also protect the rights to organize, strike, and act in solidarity. A tremendous advance would be to bring U.S. labor law into compliance. In the meantime workers are fully justified in deploying tactics of peaceful disobedience in the course of organizing, striking, and acting in solidarity.

What would it mean in practice for labor to act like a rights movement? It would not mean that unions ride back to glory on the slogan of workers' rights. Far more likely, struggles would continue to center on substantive demands, such as a fifteen-dollar minimum wage or a union contract. But a long-term commitment to workers' rights would entail basic changes not only in tactics, but conceivably in the very definition of unions as government-anointed exclusive representatives.

PEACEFUL DISOBEDIENCE AND POLITICAL ACTION would be two key components of a rights-centered strategy. When people think of civil disobedience today, most think of symbolic protests or brief disruptions designed to attract public attention. Unions have conducted some important actions of this type, for example during the San Francisco hotel strike of 2010 and the more recent Fight for Fifteen.

This kind of action is a big advance, but it does not go to the heart of the matter. There is a reason why the workers' movement, alone among progressive social movements, has been able to sustain mass organizations over a long period of time: the capacity of workers to withhold labor. Symbolic actions and consumer boycotts might extract concessions from employers who are vulnerable to public pressure—for example, fast food and retail enterprises—but even they are unlikely to accept unions (as opposed to wage hikes) solely on the basis of consumer pressure. By contrast the sit-down strikes of the 1930s succeeded because they shut down production, not only in mass production industries such as automotive and rubber manufacturing, but also in service industries such as retail and laundry.

We propose that everyone who is concerned about union revival make it a top priority to support and publicize civil disobedient exercises of workers' rights wherever and whenever they happen, especially where workers are violating restrictions on the rights to organize, strike, or act in solidarity. For example, in response to the spontaneous worker occupation of the Republic Windows factory in 2008, the United Electrical Workers Union (UE) promptly moved to support the workers and maximize the impact of their courageous action instead of worrying about possible union liability or negative reactions from politicians or employers.

A rights movement can also gain ground by campaigning for rights legislation, even if its bills fall short of passage. Consider the twentieth-century labor movement, which won all of our major national workers' rights statutes. Strikes were no more popular then than they are now. Yet for decades unions campaigned for the total abolition of anti-strike, anti-organizing, and anti-boycott laws and injunctions. Many bills were defeated, but each gave unionists an opportunity to demand the rights to organize and strike under the First Amendment freedom of association and the Thirteenth Amendment ban on involuntary servitude. And, although the provisions of the bills varied, the focus on rights remained strong until Congress finally passed the Norris-LaGuardia Anti-Injunction Act of 1932 and the National Labor Relations Act of 1935, which protected the rights to organize and strike until eroded by judicial decisions and the Taft-Hartley Act of 1947.

Compare that to the campaign for the Employee Free Choice Act of 2008–9 (EFCA), organized labor's only major effort to reform labor law in the past two decades. Right down to the title, every feature was shaped to nest comfortably in the prevailing labor law regime and dominant (anti-labor) politics. The bill declared the stirring principle that workers should have a "Free Choice" between unbridled employer domination and the crabbed version of unionism decreed by Taft-Hartley. And on the right to strike, the bill added another constraint: compulsory arbitration of first contracts. This might have made it easier for unions to sign up dues-paying members in the short run, but it would have impeded the long-run struggle. With compulsory arbitration of first contracts, organized labor would have had a hard time convincing anyone that, as Richard Trumka once put it, unions must have "their only true weapon—the right to strike."

If EFCA is an example of what not to do, then what should organized labor be doing? Endorsed by the NAACP as well as the

AFL-CIO, the Employee Empowerment Act of 2014 (EEA) would be a solid step forward. It authorizes workers who have suffered anti-union discrimination to bring a direct federal court action against their employers. In other words, it treats anti-union discrimination as a civil right, making available the remedies of the Civil Rights Act of 1964, including injunctions, compensatory damages, and punitive damages. As Tom Geoghegan, Richard Kahlenberg, and Moshe Marvit observe, the bill offers a concrete opportunity to raise and defend the proposition that labor subordination is of equivalent moral importance to racial and gender subordination. At the state level, unions might work to create and strengthen state wage boards, which, as Kate Andrias has pointed out, offer opportunities to develop sectoral bargaining outside the Taft-Hartley framework.

SO FAR WE HAVE TALKED ABOUT RIGHTS, but not about the legally structured institutions that shape the exercise of those rights. Those institutions are fatally flawed, and organized labor needs to confront that reality now, before it loses even more ground defending them.

The unionism decreed by the NLRA should be rebuilt from scratch. Although we tend to think today of the 30-plus percent union density of the 1950s as the good old days, it was not. If it becomes politically possible to amend the NLRA to make possible union revival, then it will also be possible to jettison the act's crabbed definition of unions themselves.

At the heart of the difficulty lies the system of exclusive representation. Unions that enjoy the government-conferred status of exclusive representative have little incentive and few legal avenues to build the movement as a whole.

As amended by the Taft-Hartley Act, the NLRA carves workers up into government-defined "bargaining unit" boxes, anoints a single union as the exclusive representative of the workers in any particular box, and restricts that union to bargaining over "terms and conditions of employment," a category that does not include a host of issues of vital concern to workers, including plant closings, automation, and control of pension funds. Unions stand on relatively solid legal ground when they attend to the immediate self-interest of workers in a single box, but risk employer retaliation and legal sanctions if they act on the view that the fortunes of all workers rise and fall together. For example, the flat ban on secondary boycotts blocks the workers in each bargaining unit box from acting in solidarity with workers in other boxes.

But it gets worse. Unlike corporations, which must compete in the marketplace to retain their investors, Taft-Hartley unions enjoy government-conferred monopolies over their workers. The fact that union busters repeat this point ad nauseum does not make it any less true. Once a union establishes itself as the exclusive representative in a bargaining unit, it extinguishes the freedom of workers in that unit to shift their allegiance to another union except through an arduous process of "decertification" that presents the employer with a golden opportunity to dispense with unions altogether. Union democracy can provide workers with considerable control in some settings (especially single-facility local unions, sites of some of the most vigorous popular democracy anywhere in the United States), but the law gives national union leaders enormous latitude to suppress or avoid democracy.

This kind of power presents union leaders with an almost irresistible temptation to offer, in the words of journalist and union veteran Bob Fitch, "solidarity for sale" to employers and politicians. When a union achieves the status of exclusive representative, it takes ownership of the workers' right to strike. From that point on, the union may trade the right away, and—even if it does not—the workers may be fired for striking without the union's approval. (Compare France, where the right to strike belongs to workers, not unions, and is often exercised in support of class-wide demands.) Even the most militant labor leaders typically accept a blanket no-strike clause in exchange for stability in their bargaining unit boxes, whence all dues flow. As a result most union workers are prohibited by contract from striking during all but the window periods between contracts. Because contracts expire at various times, sympathy strikes and political strikes are effectively precluded.

Exclusive representation encourages the sale of solidarity not only to employers, but also to politicians. For a vivid illustration, we need look no further than the response of labor leaders to Bernie Sanders's presidential campaign. Although neutral during the campaign, Trumka acknowledged after the fact that Sanders "elevated critical issues and strengthened the foundation of our movement." The overwhelming majority of national labor leaders, however, bowed down to the candidate backed by Wall Street, Hillary Clinton. Given the system of exclusive representation, it made sense to curry favor with the likely winner.

Exclusive representation opens the door to special restrictions on labor rights as well. Unionists routinely complain that unions are denied constitutional rights enjoyed by other voluntary associations, for example the right to engage in secondary picketing and political boycotts. But exclusive representation gives courts a plausible response, namely that because government confers the special privilege of exclusive representation on unions and not other associations, it can impose special restrictions as well.

Finally, exclusive representation undermines organized labor's claim that unionism serves as a vehicle not only for higher wages, but also for industrial democracy. At the time of Lerner's article two decades ago, nobody imagined that anti-labor interest groups would launch a successful cultural offensive against unionism, presenting themselves as defenders of democracy in the fight over EFCA (Save our secret ballot!), and of workers' constitutional rights in the campaign for the "right to work" without paying union dues.

For most unionists, resistance to the "right to work" is almost as instinctive as respect for picket lines. If a workplace is unionized, employees must pay union dues. This is justified as necessary to solve the free-rider problem. But there are plenty of solutions to that problem that do not involve forcing workers to pay dues to a union that owns their bargaining unit box solely because it mustered majority support at some point in the past. What if, for example, workers had to pay dues but could decide which union should receive the money? Similar systems have been implemented in France and Italy, where employers bargain over wages at the national level with the most representative union in the industry, but other unions compete with that union and can displace it if workers so choose.

In a political context where unions are facing an existential threat, questioning exclusive representation might seem academic. But it is not. In *Only One Thing Can Save Us* (2014), Tom Geoghegan suggests that the movement might consider bargaining away exclusive representation in exchange for rights protections such as those offered by the Employee Empowerment Act. One might disagree about the particulars, but this is the kind of discussion that the movement needs now, not only to shape the long-term campaign for legal reform, but also to inform organizing today.

If, as expected, the Supreme Court under a Trump administration strikes down the union shop in the public sector, organized labor will be presented with a challenge and opportunity to develop new systems. In states where labor remains strong, experimenting with alternatives might be possible—for example, requiring workers to pay a representation fee, but giving them a choice of organizations.

In the private sector we might put more energy into members-only or non-majority unionism. As Charles Morris has shown, a strong legal case can be made that the NLRA requires employers to bargain with non-majority unions over the wages and conditions of their members only. Earlier this year NLRB Member Kent Hirozawa agreed. And for years observers have predicted that the Board would reverse its current rule that, in the absence of an exclusive representative, a worker can be fired for insisting on bringing a representative into a disciplinary meeting. But with or without assistance from the Board, non-majority unionism offers promising opportunities to build unions outside the system of exclusive representation. After all, this was the standard path to union recognition prior to NLRA. As the best organizers testify today, their work is inevitably a process of building power in the face of employer resistance.

WE HAVE PRESENTED A SIMPLE ARGUMENT. Organized labor is being strangled by laws that block workers from exercising the rights to organize, to strike, and to act in solidarity. Unions should respond by building a rights movement, placing the struggle for those rights front and center in all movement activity, including organizing, protest, civil disobedience, political action, administrative advocacy, and litigation. In the process, the system of exclusive representation must be challenged, and labor must develop an alternative that permits broad solidarity and promotes worker freedom. We offer this proposal as a contribution to what we hope will be a productive discussion about how best to move forward in this moment of crisis and opportunity.

# Glossary of Terms

*Jen Fitzgerald*

**Product**- Body manufactured
by social assimilation in turn

produces new product
of consumption for many fingered

consumer to consume. **Boss**-
The old guard needs coddling.

Who can ever work [for]
themselves? **Documented**-

exploitable force equal to
or less than the mass of a body

accelerated toward another body.
**Body**- the means of work, the unnegotiable

negotiable, our only barrier between
the soul and the world. **Bargaining**-

Show me yours and I'll stop

lying about mine. **Laboring Body-**

a symphony. **Labor Law-** to govern
the alleged inalienable— nothing

is implicit **Workers' Rights-**
workers righting the audacity

of necessity. **Undocumented-**
See "Documented."

**Right to Strike-**
As though permission

need be granted
to uncoil the body—

release from fangs
the venom of collective.

Fitzgerald

# Why Coretta Scott King Fought for
# a Job Guarantee

*David Stein*

ON FEBRUARY 7 SENATE REPUBLICANS blocked Senator Elizabeth Warren from reading a 1986 letter by Coretta Scott King in which she opposed the nomination of Jeff Sessions to a federal bench. For Scott King, Sessions nomination to Alabama's Southern District was personal: she inveighed against his "shabby attempt to intimidate and frighten elderly black voters" and wrote that his confirmation as a federal judge would "irreparably damage the work of my husband." Had he been confirmed, Sessions would have had jurisdiction over Scott King's hometown in Perry County. Born there in 1927, she understood firsthand the violent history of such authoritarian enclaves. Her great-grandfather had been enslaved, her great-uncle lynched. Ten years old during the 1937–38 recession, she picked cotton to pay for the cost of her education. On Thanksgiving 1942, when Scott King was fifteen, their home was set ablaze. She lost her prized Bessie Smith albums in the fire and gained a visceral understanding of the depths to which white supremacists would go to maintain political, economic, and social dominance. When she was thirty-seven, the nephew of one of her closest childhood friends was beaten and killed by an Alabama state trooper, helping to inspire the historic civil rights march from Selma to Montgomery.

While a new posthumous memoir of Scott King, *My Life, My Love, My Legacy*, ghostwritten by longtime friend Barbara Reynolds, does not fully delve into the most radical aspects of Scott King's vision of social justice, the occasion of her letter being read in the Senate is a call to remember her commitment to ending all forms of violence—chief among them, the economic violence of wagelessness. Importantly, she had held these sorts of views before she met Martin, having been influenced by her involvement with the Progressive Party of the 1940s prior to her relationship with her husband. However, for fear of J. Edgar Hoover's FBI, she downplayed her own political lineage as a socialist-leaning activist. But as Scott King clarified in 1976, "I am not a ceremonial symbol—I am an activist. I didn't just emerge after Martin died—I was always there and involved." Over the course of their relationship, it might be said that Scott King pulled her husband to the left, especially on the issue of the Vietnam War.

Four days after her husband's murder on April 4, 1968, Scott King returned to Memphis to support the city's striking sanitation workers. She marched with an estimated fifty thousand people before concluding at a rally at the Memphis city hall. Amidst drizzling rain, she reminded her audience of the terrain they had traversed and the journey ahead: "We moved through . . . the period of desegregating public accommodations and on through voting rights, so that we could have political power. And now we are at the point where we must have economic power." What did that mean to her in real terms? "Every man deserves a right to a job or an income," she told the crowd of supporters.

Scott King saw economic precarity as not just a side effect of racial subjugation, but as central to its functioning. Political enfranchisement was just the first step. As she explained in 1976, "People couldn't see the economics of the movement because of the drama. . . . [The] next step was parity in income distribution." The solution Scott King promoted is an old one, but its time has come: legislation to provide federal governmental guarantees to employment, at living wages, where people are located, and in areas that serve social needs—rather than those of the market.

Such politics and values had been at the heart of black freedom movements since at least the late nineteenth century. Although many histories of welfare state development foreground the importance of Germany under Otto von Bismarck, there was also a contemporaneous black radical tradition of welfare state struggle during Reconstruction. W. E. B. Du Bois called this tradition "abolition democracy," defined as a focus on creating new democratic institutions to provide safety and social provision while also seeking to eradicate institutions of racial violence.

For Scott King the struggle for the franchise was indissolubly tied to the struggle for economic well-being and material flourishing. In practice that meant targeting the dominance of Dixiecrats in Congress, whose power had systematically limited the advance of Keynesianism across the color line. Congress's economic policies were tethered to the daily brutality of Jim Crow voter suppression, from which some of the most powerful members of Congress derived their authority. For example, on Mother's Day, 1968, Scott King and members of the Poor People's Campaign planned to target Arkansas congressman Wilbur Mills. *The Washington Post* had highlighted Mills as the "most powerful advocate" of policies that kicked mothers off of welfare and obligated them, when deemed "appropriate," to be forced to work. Mills controlled the House's Ways and Means Committee, and thus the details on major revenue bills. Widely understood as "the most important man on Capitol Hill," he was a consistent roadblock to generating greater levels of social spending that might alleviate some of the economic violence that Scott King consistently decried. By focusing protest on Mills and his fellow members of Congress, Scott King and the Mother's Day marchers were highlighting how the powerful Dixiecrats did not simply pack up their weaponized briefcases after the Voting Rights Act was passed in 1965. They retained their power on Congressional committees. Sessions's 1980s prosecutions of voting rights activists was yet another tactic to maintain political power after the Voting Rights Act. But the Voting Rights Act did provide a means for advancing the political power of the black freedom movement. And in the decades after her husband's assassination Scott King wholly dedicated herself to using the vote to this end.

In 1974 Scott King co-founded the National Committee for Full Employment/Full Employment Action Council (NCFE/FEAC) to fight for legislation that guaranteed jobs for all Americans. Guaranteed jobs for all who wanted them—regardless of race or gender—had long been a goal of Scott King's and the black freedom movement. But in a time of rising inflation and unemployment, and fearing a growing backlash against the civil rights agenda, Scott King believed that guaranteed jobs were also necessary to mollify fears of economic competition on the part of white workers. In the 1940s her father's sawmill was burned to the ground two weeks after its opening, following his refusal to sell to it to a white man. She knew that shared feelings of precarity could provoke racist violence just as much as they might elicit solidarity. Scott King's struggle for guaranteed jobs to anyone who wanted one was as tactical as it was moral.

In current debates, demands for guaranteed jobs and demands for a basic income are often framed as diametrically opposed. But for Scott King and the broader black freedom movement, these were coupled together. Scott King was an ardent advocate for the National Welfare Rights Organization's calls for a guaranteed annual income (which, in contrast to some basic income schemes, always emphasized the need for a cash benefit of a living wage). But she spent more time campaigning for guaranteed jobs. In these proposals, there were income guarantees that would be provided for those who are unable to work due to age, ability, or care-giving responsibilities. The goal was to expand the welfare state through social movement victories, not impose workfare.

It is also important to note that "full employment" for Scott King did not mean what it more commonly means today: a certain percentage of unemployment that economists and policymakers deem necessary in order to keep inflation at bay. As this conceptualization of "full employment" was taking hold, NCFE/FEAC denounced this style of public policy. The organization described it as an "unconscionable view that the evils imposed by unemployment upon scores of millions of people whose breadwinners are unemployed are acceptable in the name of restraining inflation." Scott King and NCFE/FEAC insisted that full employment meant that the government needed to provide a good job to all who wanted one.

Likewise, NCFE/FEAC pursued a path away from the types of military Keynesianism that had become entrenched after the failure of the Progressive Party in the 1940s. As Scott King explained in 1975, "This nation has never honestly dealt with the question of a peacetime economy." For her, economic well-being could no longer rely on build-ing weapons for the military industrial complex. Just as her husband had emphasized the importance of safe and dignified work through his support for Memphis's sanitation workers, Scott King showed her support for human services by marching alongside the black women hospital workers of Charleston, South Carolina, during their 113-day strike in 1969.

Scott King's vision of full employment emphasized jobs for social needs. "We are going to have to create meaningful jobs. . . . Jobs that would serve some human need. . . . As long as there are people you are going to have certain health care needs, educational needs, things that you know will make for a better quality of living." She believed that it was essential to move beyond jobs "that were really created with the profit-making motive." Accordingly NCFE/FEAC called for jobs programs to create housing for all; to encourage environmental conservation; to build mass transportation; and to provide more funding for the arts, cultural, and recreational programming. The organization sought to reduce the amount of time people worked, without a reduction in pay.

To do this, Scott King and NCFE/FEAC focused on shaping legislation. They were the grassroots force behind the Humphrey-Hawkins Full Employment Act of 1978. To support the bill, NCFE/FEAC's organized a "Full Employment Action Week" in 1977. They mobilized more than 1.5 million people in protests and actions in three hundred cities. Sixty thousand people turned out to the rally in Buffalo, New York. Another forty thousand people attended the full employment parade in Erie, Pennsylvania. NCFE/FEAC worked alongside groups such as the National Council of Churches to create local organizations in Boston, Denver, Columbus, Des Moines, St. Louis, and other cities. The leadership of the Council of Churches echoed Scott King's assessments during the week of action, saying that the federal government should serve as the "employer of last resort" to create jobs in "energy, mass transportation, housing, education, [and] health care."

But these efforts were not enough. On the treacherous road from bill to law, the most innovative aspects of that law were stripped away.

Provisions such as the creation of a legally enforceable right to a job—with a national planning mechanism to achieve this—were victims of intense opposition from the Business Roundtable and National Association of Manufacturers. Consequently, as Americans for Democratic Action reported to its members at the time, the Senate Banking Committee "did a real hatchet job on the bill." Although forced to compromise with some of the provisions in the Banking Committee's version of the bill, the new law still demanded that unemployment be reduced to 3 percent by 1983 and that the Federal Reserve now give biannual testimony to Congress on how the Fed was working to achieve these goals (since the Fed had been effectively ignoring its mandate to facilitate maximum employment since the 1950s). For Scott King, this partial victory was not the end, but one point in a longer journey.

Scott King's struggles to create guaranteed jobs programs continue to hold resonance for today. What is the meaning of civil rights victories in the face of persistent unemployment? "The conscious politically motivated economic policies of the past few years that are keeping large numbers of Americans unemployed, especially blacks, are nothing less than a frontal assault on the gains and victories of the civil rights movement," she said during the Full Employment Action Week. "What good is the legal right to sit in a restaurant if one cannot afford the price of food? What good is the promise of fair employment when there is no employment for black Americans?" These questions endure in this era of economic inequality: the Movement for Black Lives has similarly demanded guaranteed jobs. The Coalition of Black Trade Unionists, whose leaders in the 1970s had worked alongside NCFE/FEAC, continues its longstanding efforts in this area. Each group carries on the legacy of black working-class political formations developing radical and expansive solutions to the problems of its era.

Others draw explicitly on Scott King's legacy. In addition to Senator Warren's efforts to bring Scott King's voice to the debates around Sessions, the Center for Popular Democracy's Fed Up campaign is keeping the goal of full employment on the table. On February 15 the organization's "Full Employment Defenders" headed to Congress to attend Federal Reserve Chair Janet Yellen's biannual "Humphrey-Hawkins" testimony—a key remnant of the 1978 law. However, in 1979, only a year after the law was passed, under Federal Reserve Chairman Paul Volcker, the hearings bordered on farcical, with Volcker asserting that controlling inflation should continue to take precedence over the Fed's employment mandate—a direct contravention of the NCFE/FEAC's goals. The infamous "Volcker Shock" then raised interests rates to heretofore-unfathomable levels and helped bring rates of unemployment for black workers to as high as 19.5 percent in 1983. And too often since, this attitude—that puts fears of inflation above the lives of unemployed people—has guided the Fed's policy. But Fed Up is using the tools Scott King helped create—such as the Fed's own testimony before legislators—to try to change that.

As Shawn Sebastian, Fed Up's Co-Director, told me, "Coretta Scott King's vision of full employment is sophisticated in its targets but also ultimately viscerally relevant to the lives of everyday people, particularly people of color. . . . Scott King created a handle on this lever of power at the Federal Reserve that was designed to be remote and inaccessible that I like to think we have been able to grab onto a few generations later." And for Sebastian and his comrades, the goal of full employment has been able to guide them as the Trump agenda coalesces. As he explained, "[Trump's] broader push to deregulate the banks has shifted everything, but Full Employment remains our lodestar. . . . We've used the [goal] of Full Employment that Coretta Scott King created decades ago to be a compass as we navigate an uncertain future. Coretta Scott King's sharp analysis and moral clarity continue to guide us."

What will Scott King's legacy look like when and if the Coalition of Black Trade Unionists, the Movement for Black Lives, Fed Up, and their allies are successful in achieving governmental guarantees to jobs and income? A moment of victory can suddenly recast the past history of losses. Scott King and NCFE/FEAC sowed seeds that needed time and cultivation to eventually flower. During a time of drought, nevertheless, these seeds persist.

# From *SPEECH*

## *Jill Magi*

Still the unequal
distribution of life and death
speaks
still stuttering the gap
between hope and harm
    still an ear
to the pitch of endurance
or exhaustion which you?

    As an event broadcasts over
murmurs of daily chronic cruddy suffering
she walks across a parking lot
toward a home not like a shared body
but a shared body looping through
her black chiffon
his white linen his blue cotton her
uniform flowing an enfleshment
made mutual she touches
the string of theirs pulling
close to the beat of them
pliable
a sternum a cavity variously

inheriting a stress
a social constraint
a binding of not Europe
while Europe says "their future
can never be a future"
the genealogical afternoon adhan
tumbles through the alley
between the pharmacy
and her skin shedding
its autology

     Comes the green
afternoon window light spreading
she thinks safely of her freedom tied to a man
whose coveralls hang from his shoulders
in the sun whose fabric of striped tape
reflects the lights around him as he works
in the median picking up
tissues
     how would democracy lift him
out of the heat
how would absolute monarchy
lift him out of the danger
of traffic pounding in two directions?

     When the light turned red
she brought the housing project
into her thoughts through her mouth
an emblem making a city
     a memory called Something Green

to denote the garden it wanted to be
where they desired to walk and sit
but learned how to keep on how to
cut out cut up masterfully and stand
always ready

        I mean we swallow all
at the light where cars pull off highways
to pick up drugs for fun we know
the news drives back to the suburbs
we know the report provides a number
of those shot dead their person being
a weekend elsewhere being days off being
out of their minds

          recreation link death
          disposable income link death
          extra time link extra death

A city rejects repair
does not form a task force to stop it
        so to call a town friendly
draw a dotted line below your neck below your
smile is a school district a real estate name
redrawn renamed so as to drain
for profit for one idea of fun

        I mean to say that most
do not believe in equality and will advocate
for less worth versus their progeny more

Magi

# Bargaining

*Jen Fitzgerald*

The Ask: Employees may never fall ill.
The Get: Workers beg, barter, beat bodies
out of sick. The Ask: Never an injury
on the line. The Get: Workmen's comp
shattered like porcelain; broken bones
and limps hidden. The Ask: Four children
to lock in desperation; they may never fall
ill. The Get: Who-comes-in-where blame
game—cook little brother breakfast, don't
wake them, anger them. The Ask: We just
want quiet, a labor force of yes, American
Dream, day dream, dream a little dream,
old time religion, don't stop believing,
muscle, sports, madness, spit shined, moon
shined, good-natured consent. The Get: This.

# CONTRIBUTORS

*Ammiel Alcalay* teaches at Queens College and the Graduate Center at the City University of New York. He is the author of *a little history*.

*Roy Bahat* is the head of Bloomberg Beta, a venture capital firm, and the co-chair of the Shift Commission on Work, Workers, and Technology.

*Peter Barnes* is a cofounder of Credo Mobile, an advisor to the Roosevelt Institute, and author of *With Liberty and Dividends for All*.

*Annette Bernhardt* is director of the Project on Low-Wage Work at the UC Berkeley Labor Center and co-editor of *The Gloves-Off Economy*.

*Juliana Bidadanure* is Assistant Professor in Political Philosophy at Stanford and is on the advisory board of Stanford's McCoy Family Center for Ethics in Society.

*Ed Bruno* is former director of the United Electrical Radio and Machine Workers of America and past southern director for the National Nurses Union.

*Diane Coyle* teaches at the University of Manchester and is author of *GDP: A Brief but Affectionate History*.

*Patrick Diamond* is a Visiting Fellow at Kellogg College, Oxford, and lectures at Queen Mary, University of London. He is the author of *Endgame for the Centre-Left: The Retreat of European Social Democracy*.

*Jen Fitzgerald* is a community organizer and author of *The Art of Work*.

*David McDermott Hughes* is Professor of Anthropology at Rutgers University and author of *Whiteness in Zimbabwe*.

*Peter Kellman* works with the Movement Building/Education Committee of the Maine AFL-CIO and is author of *Building Unions: Past, Present and Future*.

*Jill Magi* is an artist, critic, and author of *LABOR*.

*James Gray Pope* is Professor of Law and Sidney Reitman Scholar at Rutgers University.

*Connie Razza* is director of Strategic Research at the Center for Popular Democracy.

*David Rolf* is president of Seattle's Local 775 chapter of the SEIU and author of *The Fight for Fifteen*.

*Brishen Rogers* is Associate Professor of Law at Temple University.

*Tommie Shelby* is Caldwell Titcomb Professor of African and African American Studies and of Philosophy at Harvard University and the author of *Dark Ghettos*.

*David Stein* is a Lecturer in African American Studies and History at UCLA. His book *Fearing Inflation, Inflating Fears: The Civil Rights Struggle for Full Employment and the Rise of the Carceral State, 1929–1986* is forthcoming from UNC Press.

*Philippe van Parijs* is Professor of Economic and Social Ethics at the University of Louvain and co-author of *Basic Income: A Radical Proposal for a Free Society and a Sane Economy*.

*Dorian Warren* is a Fellow at the Roosevelt Institute and Board Chair of the Center for Community Change. His books *The Three Faces of Unions* and *Boxing Out* are forthcoming.

*Corrie Watterson* is Senior Researcher for SEIU 775 in Seattle and contributed to *The Fight for Fifteen*.